FEEDING the ENEMY

FEEDING the ENEMY

Soviet Women in Nazi Labor Camps in Norway

LIV MJELDE

Aristata Press

Project coordinators: Judy Blankenship and Andrew Wilson
Cover and Jacket Design: Anne McClard

ISBN 979-8-9906293-6-3 (paper)
979-8-9906293-7-0 (e-book)
Library of Congress Control Number: 2025918754

First published as: *Saksens Hemmelighet: Russerjenters Arbeid, Liv Og Fødsler i Fangeleirer I Nord, 1942-1945*
Svein Sandnes bokforlag 2018.
Original English translation: Bibbi Lee

The writer has received support from the Norwegian Non-Fiction Literary Fund.

The Nordland Museum's contribution of photos and graphics from its collection is gratefully acknowledged.

Cover photo: Women in front of the barracks, Langstranda prison camp, May 1945, photographer unknown.

Aristata Press, Portland, Oregon
http://aristatapress.com

To my mother and father
for their love and lessons in life and politics

"Love, work and knowledge are the cornerstones of life. They should also govern it." Wilhelm Reich, *Listen Little Man* (1948)

CONTENTS

PRINCIPAL CHARACTERS

Yuri: Yuri Fedorovich Salnikov was born to Russian prisoners of war Fedor and Galina at Langstranda, close to Bodø, northern Norway, in December 1944. For reasons described in this book, he was officially registered as having been born in 1947 in Vladivostok. He lived much of his early life in Klaipeda, Lithuania, before moving to St. Petersburg, where he met his wife Natalya in 1969 and began his successful career as an artist. His son Mikhail was born in 1975. Yuri finally revisited the town of his birth in 2008.

Fedor: Fedor Vasilievitch Savin (later changed to Salnikov), Yuri's father, was born in Siberia in 1918. An electrician who was conscripted into the Soviet army in 1939, Fedor was captured by the German army in September 1941 at the Battle of Kyiv and transferred to a prison camp near Bodø. Repatriated in 1945, he was first sent to Vladivostok before moving to Klaipeda in 1951, where he died in 1987.

Galina: Galina Valentinovna Korolenko, Yuri's mother, was born in Leningrad (now St. Petersburg) in 1925. She was abducted by the German army in October 1942 in Artemki, close to the town of Gzhatsk (now Gargarin) and taken to work in the Frostfilet factory in

Langstranda. She was repatriated with the six-month-old Yuri in mid-1945 and followed Fedor to Vladivostok in 1946, where they had a second child. She died in 1992.

Anny: Hanna Evensen (née Koljada) was born in October 1924 in Dnipropetrovsk (now Dnipro), Ukraine. She was abducted in May 1942 and transported to work in the filleting factory at Hammerfest the following month. There she met Jacob Evensen, a young Norwegian worker. In November 1944, she and 150 other Soviet women were transferred to a different factory in Svolvær, and then transferred to Bodø in the spring. She married Jacob following the end of the war and returned to Hammerfest, where she lived until her death in 2022.

Marfa: Marija "Marfa" Maksimova Stepina was born in 1927 in Smolensk, Russia. She was abducted near the city of Bryansk around the same time as Galina. While at Frostfilet, she formed an attachment with another Russian, Arkady Mozerin, with whom she had her daughter, Valentina, while still in Norway. She and Arkady were unable to get together following repatriation to Russia. She died in Bryansk in February 2017.

Valentina: Valentina Stepina was born to Marfa and Arkady in late 1944, originally under the given name of Tatyana. She returned with her mother to Bryansk in 1945. After many years of hardship and stigma due to her birth in Norway, she was able to receive a small pension funded by the German state, in recognition of having been born in a German prison camp. She attended a 2015 commemoration of the repatriation in Luleå, Sweden, but has not yet been able to revisit Norway.

MAPS

Northern Europe 1945

Nordic Countries and Soviet Union 1945

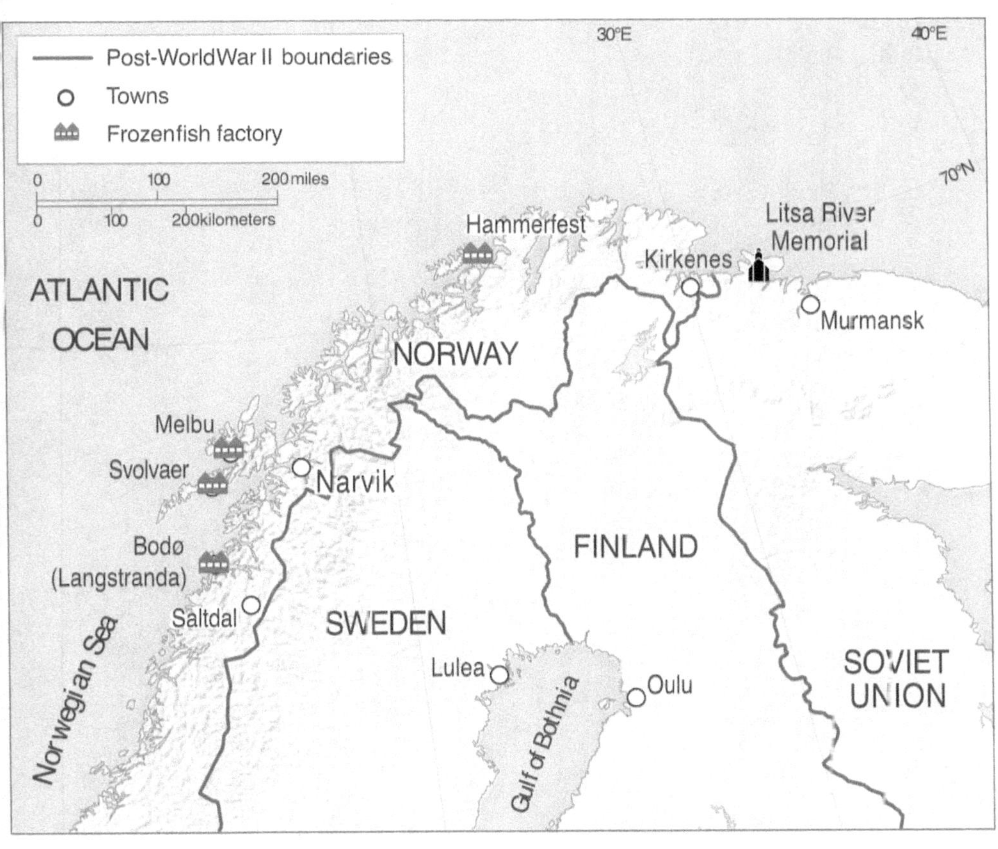

INTRODUCTION

The spark that led me to write this story was a chance meeting with a young man in St. Petersburg in September 2005. He asked for help finding his father's birthplace, which he believed had been in Norway during World War II. However, the family had no documentation from Norway regarding his birth. Nobody knew where he was born or what his parents had been doing in Norway.

The search for a Soviet child born somewhere in Norway laid the groundwork for my immersion into a long-buried story: the history of Soviet women forced into slave labor in northern Norway's fish factories during World War II.

In today's culture of public commemorations, this part of our history has been marginalized and largely erased. During the Cold War, Norwegian authorities relocated or destroyed Soviet graves and memorials. Archives and records from the occupation period of 1940 to 1945 were eliminated, and people were silenced, especially in northern Norway. The silence surrounding these stories motivated me to dig deeper into their wartime lives. Many of the stories uncovered during my research did not align with the official accounts of Norwegian heroism in opposing the Nazi occupiers.

What happened to this chapter in the history of the war? Was there a deliberate decision to forget the presence and repatriation of Soviet prisoners? Their contribution to Norwegian industry during World War II is scarcely mentioned in Norway's "official history," the mainstream narrative of those tragic years. The historian Gunnar D. Hatlehol argues that, during the post-war years, the academic world showed little interest in foreign World War II prisoners. The exception was the writer Helge Krog, who raised the subject in his 1945 book *The Sixth Column? On Norwegian Industry's Contribution to Nazi Germany's Warfare*. His publisher, Aschehoug, a venerable and respected enterprise, declined to publish it at the time. Krog self-published his book, and it was republished by Pax Publishing House in 1969.

It is only recently that the fate of Soviet prisoners in Norway during World War II has been documented, especially regarding their contributions to various Norwegian industries and transport systems. As is so often the case, official history paid little attention to the role of women.

My professional experience as a researcher has influenced how and why this book came to be written. But I also have personal reasons for engaging with the story. As well as my experience as a child in wartime Norway (see chapter 1) my connections go further afield, including to members of my extended family as far away as Canada. One of these connections is to my grandmother-in-law, Muriel Chillingwood Colls Reid, who started writing a political diary in that fateful year, 1933.

Muriel was born in Kent, England, on March 20, 1887, and emigrated to Canada in 1905. She was a child of her times, but a woman of quite independent ideas inspired by her suffragette mother. From Vancouver, Muriel followed the interwar years with critical British eyes, commenting on the horrors of the rise of Nazism. In an entry from 1934, she wrote of the infamous Night of the Long Knives when Adolf Hitler orchestrated the killing of his old comrade in arms, Ernst Röhm, along with dozens—possibly hundreds—of his followers in the SA (Sturmabteilung, the paramilitary force most commonly known as the Brownshirts). Muriel asks the question: "How did the Germans elect a man as mad as Caligula as their dictator?" Conscious that the newspapers' focus on a few men's short-term actions ignored their long-term consequences for the rest of the population, she ends the paragraph with words that today seem prophetic: "Poor German women."

Though separated by almost a century, I keenly empathize with Muriel's concerns about women, politics, and ideology, both in Northern Europe where I live and in countries far beyond Norway's borders. These issues have been a central concern in my work as a sociologist and academic, particularly my writing in the sociology of education. My research has taught me that the roles assigned to women in life are influenced by shifting ideologies. In particular, consideration of the division of labor and gender reveals both to be social constructs that fluctuate along with economic and political conditions. This theme runs through my work like the proverbial red thread, and has been one of my primary concerns throughout my career since the 1970s. It is one of the reasons I was so drawn to this hidden history, which highlighted a seeming contradiction: the Nazi occupiers' use of Soviet women as slave labor in the Norwegian fishing industry despite Nazism's general insistence on women's roles as baby-breeders and as homemakers for men.

Memory is socially constructed, with different emphases prevailing at different times and the process coming under constant challenge. Which stories are told and which are silenced, in wider society and in our private lives, depends greatly on the political climate. The French philosopher and historian Ernest Renan pointed out in 1882 that national narratives are constructed as much of amnesia as of memory. In *1984*, George Orwell reminds us of what the powerful have always known: "Who controls the past controls the future; who controls the present controls the past." In recent years, both the silences and the heroic stories have been exposed to new research, revealing more complex stories surrounding the Norwegian resistance as well as collaboration during the war years. This book has been nourished by the new knowledge as well as my own research into gender questions and feminist scholarship during the past fifty years.

Inevitably, the narrative defies simple chronology, and I hope the reader will accompany me as I pursue the various strands of the overall story:

Part 1 opens in St. Petersburg, where we began to unravel the mysteries connected with Yuri Salnikov and his family.

Part 2 deals with Adolf Hitler's vision of a Europe transformed to meet the needs of the Thousand Year Reich and how Norway's fishing industry fit into this vision. It also explores how captured women from the occupied Soviet territories became part of this story.

Part 3 describes the everyday life in the factories in Bodø in Nordland County, in Hammerfest close to the North Cape in Finnmark, and in Melbu in the Vesterålen Archipelago.

Part 4 depicts the course of the German retreat beginning in 1944, which included the move of the Hammerfest fish factory south.

Part 5 covers the liberation of Norway and the repatriation of the Soviet prisoners.

Finally, Part 6 takes us to the Swedish city of Luleå in 2015, where the seventieth anniversary of the repatriation was commemorated.

The Norwegian edition of this book, published in 2018, was thirteen years in the making. The English version was in process for another seven years. It is thus a work that was always in progress, and both my knowledge and the text have been under development all the time. Many people have helped along the way (see the Acknowledgments), but I particularly wish to note my Canadian husband, Richard Heywood Daly, who has been an important part of the process since that first, serendipitous meeting in St. Petersburg two decades ago.

Liv Mjelde

Oslo, May 5, 2025

PART I

STORIES WITHIN STORIES

1

"MY FATHER WAS BORN IN NORWAY" (ST. PETERSBURG, 2005)

On a sunny autumn afternoon in 2005, while visiting St. Petersburg, the former capital of Imperial Russia, my husband and I stepped into an elegant gift shop nestled within the Stroganov Palace. The palace, a grand confection of pink- and lemon-hued baroque opulence, commands a central position on Nevsky Prospekt, the principal thoroughfare of a city that has borne many names—St. Petersburg, Petrograd, Leningrad, and, finally, St. Petersburg once more. Constructed for the illustrious Stroganov family in the 1700s, it arose during Peter the Great's ambitious transformation of the city into Russia's glittering showcase and a gateway to the world, opening trade routes through the Baltic Sea. By the time of our visit in 2005, the palace housed a chocolate museum, a souvenir shop, and an art gallery displaying the works of contemporary Russian painters.

A young man named Mikhail, who worked in the shop, welcomed us warmly and asked about our origins. When we told him we were from Oslo, Norway, he shared that his father had been born in Norway in late December of 1944, though he did not know the exact location. I assumed that his father was born to a Soviet father and a Norwegian mother, and I asked if that was the case. To my surprise, Mikhail explained that his grandparents were both Soviet citizens. I knew that Norway had been home to tens of thousands of Yugoslav, Polish, and Soviet male prisoners during the Nazi occupation, but I had never encountered stories involving women prisoners.

I am a child of that war. Born on August 29, 1939—just two days before Nazi troops invaded Poland—I spent my earliest years in occupied Oslo, the capital of Norway. My childhood was marked by the rhythms of occupation: the tramp of marching soldiers, the wail of air raid sirens, and the terrifying explosions of bombs and grenades. I recall long, uneasy nights huddled with my family and neighbors in the dank, rat-infested cellar beneath our apartment building in Oslo's East End. The German Wehrmacht had seized our local school, the very place where I later began my first seven years of education. Occasionally, when bombing was expected (the bombs of Britain's Royal Air Force, targeting the German military), my parents sent me to relatives in the countryside. It was on one of those rural visits that I was woken by arrival of German soldiers and dogs to arrest my uncle—an experience that has stuck with me for life.

Soviet prisoners being marched to work in Trondenes, Norway. (Photo: Trondenes Historic Center.)

Soldiers were a constant presence in our lives—ubiquitous, smiling at children, and offering sweets. I quickly learned how to say *No*. I also have vivid memories of prisoners of war, guarded by German soldiers and fearsome German shepherd dogs, herded through the streets near my home. Each morning, these prisoners were marched down Schweigaards Street, where I lived, en route from the Etterstad camp in eastern Oslo to worksites scattered across the city. Their labor was grueling—unloading freight at the port and shifting supplies at the Grønlia food storage depot in central Oslo. At day's end, the weary men were marched back to Etterstad under the watchful eyes of their captors.

I remember the rhythmic clatter of tram number 6, which ran from Etterstad to Skøyen, passing one side of our apartment building. On the other side, freight trains rumbled out of Oslo. Sometimes the trams carried prisoners and their German guards into the city for special tasks. The trains, however, bore darker cargo—prisoners transported in open cars to camps across Norway. Many of these prisoners were taken by train to Trondheim in central Norway and from there by boat to the forbidding reaches of northern Norway.

Mikhail asked if we might help uncover the true place of his father's birth. This inquiry became my gateway into a chapter of Norwegian history unfamiliar to me and most Norwegians. Among the approximately 9,000 forced laborers sent to Norway from the Soviet Union—distinct from the far larger number of prisoners of war—were some 1,400 women and an additional 400 children, aged fifteen and younger.

Mikhail knew only fragments of his family's story. His grandmother, originally from Leningrad, had given birth to his father in Norway during the war's final phase, but no records survived to mark the date or place. On a scrap of paper, he carefully noted the scant details he had.

SaLNiKOV
Fedor & GaLiNA
(G. Father & mother)
SaLNiKOV Yuary
(Father)
was born 1945

Once back in Norway, I began contacting individuals I hoped might assist in tracing the birthplace of Yuri Salnikov during the final year of the occupation. My first contact was the late poet, historian, and teacher Dag Skogheim, who lived in Levanger, a small town just northwest of Trondheim. Dag responded to my email immediately, offering encouragement but also issuing a somber caution:

> It is the unfortunate truth that most of the material remains buried in darkness or obscurity. The Cold War brutally rendered everything a taboo. You have rocky ground to plough, and I wish you good luck in this incredibly exciting field.

Dag advised that I begin the search for Yuri and his parents at Falstad, a former Nazi prison camp now transformed into the Falstad Memorial and Human Rights Center, inaugurated in 2000. Located roughly an hour's drive north of Trondheim in central Norway, the center serves as both an educational hub and a site of historical documentation focused on wartime imprisonment.

Originally built in 1921 as a reform school for delinquent boys, Falstad was seized by the German SS in 1941 and repurposed into Norway's second-largest *Strafgefangenenlager* (prison camp). Between 1941 and 1945, approximately 5,000 individuals were detained there, most of them Norwegian political prisoners. For many, Falstad was a temporary stop en route to the Grini camp near Oslo—and often, from there, to concentration camps in Germany.

Falstad also witnessed the deportation of Jewish prisoners from Trondheim to Auschwitz, as well as the incarceration of foreign captives from the Soviet Union, Yugoslavia, Poland, and Denmark. Executions took place in Falstad Forest, about one kilometer from the camp, where an estimated one hundred Soviet and seventy-four Yugoslav prisoners of war, along with forty-three Norwegian political prisoners, met their deaths.

The treatment of Soviet prisoners constitutes a tragic and little-known chapter of the war in Norway. Between 1941 and 1945, some 100,000 Soviet prisoners of war and forced laborers were brought to

Norway, where they built roads, railways, and fortifications in the unforgiving Norwegian climate. Subjected to subsistence rations, inadequate clothing, and brutal treatment, an estimated 13,700 died of starvation and disease or exposure in the five hundred or so prison camps scattered across the country, with the northern regions being particularly grueling. The number of Soviet citizens who died under these conditions exceeded the total number of Norwegians—an estimated 10,000—killed during the entire war. Yet, despite being buried in Norwegian soil, these Belarussians, Russians, Ukrainians, and others remain excluded from the nation's collective memory of the occupation.

Liberated Soviet prisoners of war muster at dockside in Langstranda for their journey back to the USSR on the SS Mungo. *(Photo courtesy Nordlands Museum.)*

When at last liberation came in May 1945, many Soviet prisoners were still in Norway. As prison gates swung open, captives spilled into the streets—and into the homes—of ordinary Norwegians. They shared what little they had: the Norwegians from their meager supplies and the prisoners from stores abandoned by retreating German forces. Bonds of friendship and love were forged, and nine months later, the consequences of these brief encounters emerged.

To this day, children born in wartime Norway continue to search for their families across the former Soviet Union. For decades, separated by the Iron Curtain, such reunions were little more than impossible dreams. Yet the echoes of those connections persist, reverberating across time and borders.

On March 12, 1947, President Harry S. Truman identified the Soviet Union as the new enemy, a stance solidified by the inauguration of NATO on April 4, 1949. These developments effectively erased the fate of Soviet prisoners of war from both public consciousness and Norwegian national history. During the Cold War, World War II was reinterpreted through the prism of what the Norwegian historian Steiner Aas described as the "memory politics" of the era. Successive "memory agents"—governments, organizations, and individuals—crafted narratives to serve their respective agendas.

In Norway, the focus on Soviet prisoners of war during the Nazi occupation was replaced by stories about their postwar fate upon returning to the Soviet Union. They were no longer viewed as victims of Nazism but as victims of Stalinism, with Cold War political priorities overshadowing the solidarity of the wartime alliance. No resources were dedicated to studying these prisoners' experiences in Norway's labor camps; their lives during captivity were deemed unworthy of scholarly or public interest.

Even more troubling than this indifference was the deliberate historical erasure known as Operation Asphalt—another dark chapter in Norway's wartime history, whose implications for Yuri's story are explored in chapter 17. This policy of neglect and erasure appeared to shift after the fall of the Berlin Wall in 1989. Yet today, efforts to recover these forgotten histories continue to face significant challenges.

It was a stroke of luck that just a year before I met Mikhail in St. Petersburg, the researcher Marianne Neerland Soleim had provided the first solid quantitative documentation on Soviet prisoners of war in Norway—including, crucially, the female prisoners. Her groundbreaking doctoral dissertation at the University of Tromsø, *Soviet Pris-*

oners of War in Norway in the Period 1941–45: Their Numbers, Organization, and Repatriation, proved invaluable. It offered critical insights and provided many clues in our search for Yuri Salnikov's birthplace.

When I contacted Marianne, she unearthed records in the Norwegian Digital Archives documenting the 1945 departure of prisoners of war from Narvik. Among the names she found were those of Yuri and his parents.

Narvik had served as the central gathering point for Soviet prisoners of war from Norway's northern counties, Troms and Nordland. Linked by rail to Sweden's vital iron-ore mines in Kiruna—and from there to the Baltic coast—it provided a route for repatriation. In the summer of 1945, a total of 24,339 Soviet citizens traveled this path, returning home via Sweden and Finland to the Soviet Union. Yuri and his parents were almost certainly among them. Yet the archives yielded no clues about their earlier movements—the place of Yuri's birth or the locations where his parents had been held remained unrecorded.

This new research, however, eventually enabled me to answer Mikhail Salnikov's question. On October 20, 2005, I sent a letter to St. Petersburg enclosing copies of the archival lists. There, the names of Mikhail's father and grandparents appeared:

> ***Yuri Fedorovitsj Korolenko****, January 1, 1945, registration number 2141025.*
>
> ***Galina Korolenko Valentinova****, mother, January 1, 1925, registration number 2140823.*
>
> ***Fedor Vasil'evitsj Savin****, father, January 1, 1918, registration number 2140924.*

Why did they all share the same birthdate? For reasons now obscured by the fog of war and bureaucracy, prisoners were often registered with January 1 as their date of birth—a standardized practice that was arbitrary yet practical for administrative purposes.

It wasn't much, yet it was momentous. The records confirmed what Mikhail had long suspected—his father had indeed been born in Norway during the final tumultuous months of 1944. The Great Patriotic War, as World War II is known in Russia, had brought Galina and Fedor to a fateful encounter somewhere in Norway, setting in motion the events that shaped their complex and secretive life together.

I considered my task complete, but another journey to St. Petersburg the following year rekindled my curiosity and compelled me to delve even deeper.

U VI RUSSELAGER FABRIK FROSTFILET. /barn/ BARN født Liste 1945

Nr.	Navn	Fødselsaar		Far	Mor
1.	Valentin	19/1	1945	Driga Alexandr	Grossva Irina
2.	Ljubov	30/3	-"-	Jakubovskij Stanislav	Savina Sinaida
3.	Evgenij	3/4	-"-	Skinuk Aleksandr	Valjakova Nadja
~~4.~~	~~Sereda~~				
4.	Nadja	25/2	-"-	Sereda Stepan	Burova Praskovja
5.	Evgenij	17/8	1944	Rubskovskij Vasilij	Sedneva Sinaida
6.	Peter	19/10	-"-	Pogerelskuk Evgenij	Pavlutina Tatjana
7.	Konstantin	1/1	1945	Anisskenko Aleksej	Popova Ekaterina
8.	Marija	14/5	-"-	Skvosnukov Grigorij	Prisadova Evgenija
9.	Boris	20/2	-"-	Kruskovskij Viktor	Kostjasina Polina
10.	Leonid	17/10	1944	Sensov Peter	Alexashina Olga
11.	Grigorij	3/3	1945	Vojasko Kiril	Kovaleva Nastja
12.	Valentin	24/1	1942	Bolgarev Boris	Bondareva Tamara
13.	Svetlana	29/1	-"-	Tretnej Stepan	Potjahajlo Sanja
14.	Raisa	17/3	-"-	h a n s	Savesenova Marija
15.	Soja	19/8	1944	Beresnuk Vasilij	Babanova Nastja
16.	Pelegeja	7/1	1945	Sepetuk Timofej	Seveleva Elena
17.	Anatolij	14/1	-"-	Tretjakov Semen	Ivaskova Tamara
18.	Evgenij	5/1	1944	Tkask Mishail	Kireeva Katerina
19.	Jurij	1/1	1945	Salnikov Feodor	Korolenko Halina
20.	Evgenija	5/1	-"-	Selesnov Aleksandr	Asorenko Aleksandra
21.	Wladimir	25/3	1944	Krivobjakov Mishail	Maksanova Elena
22.	Anatolij	1/7	-"-	Dosohoj Vladimir	Maksanova Varvara
23.	Ludmila	24/9	-"-	Batosskov Viktor	Koslova Antonina
24.	Viktor	5/10	-"-	Stepanov Peter	Krilova Evdokija
25.	Lubov	14/9	-"-	Soroka Sergej	Arbusova Anna
26.	Elesoveta	25/9	-"-	Boturin Peter	Mosaeva Polina
27.	Valentina	18/11	-"-	Isskuk Ivan	Efrenova Klavdija
28.	Nina.	28/8	-"-	Savskuk Vladimir	Liljakova Marija
29.	Viktor	27/8	-"-	Dmitrenko Anatolij	Krivenkova Ekaterina
30.	Svetlana	27/10	-"-	Dereska Jacop	Troshova Albina
31.	Soja	17/7	-"-	Vojtuk Peter	Mesakina Marija
32.	Vasilij	24/8	-"-	Pavluk Sergej	Kasjanova Ekaterina
33.	Nikolaj	24/7	-"-	Miroaniskenko Ivan	Babkova Sinaida
34.	Alexandr	8/10	-"-	Dubovoj Ivan	Majorova Tanja
35.	Anatolij	11/3	1945	Berasskinskij Andrej	Kovaleva Polina
36.	Anna	4/5	-"-	~~Lapenkova~~ Kaplun	Lapenkova Elena
37.	Nikolaj	12/6	1944	Tkaskuk Vladimir	Nekiskena Marija
38.	Viktor	24/10	-"-	Beresovoi Demitrij	Poskenaeva Anna
39.	Nadesda	18/10	-"-	Domenik Viktor	Lukutena Vera
40.	Vladimer	27/10	-"-	Kobilkin Ivan	Saizeva Marija
41	Alexandr	4/4	-"-	Tristakenko Michail	Palekova Tatjana
42:	Valentina	28/5	-"-	Simikov Nikolai	Lakuzova Nadesda
43.	Sfija	31/11	-"-	Lisakov Ivan	Bozai Elena
44.	Nikolai	18/9	-"-	Danskenko Vasilij	Miljanama Marija
45.	Nina	1/10	-"-	Artkomenko Vasilij	Sucharukova Marija
46.	Evhenij	12/3	1945	Driha Vasilij	Chranoleva Tamara
47.	Raisa	5/3	-"-	Novikov Petr	Savskenko Olja
48.	Valentin	20/4	1944	Bespalskuk Anton	Sukova Tatjana
49.	Vladimer	3/12	-"-	Ribaskuk Vladimir	Soloduchina Evdokija
50.	Vitalij	19/10	-"-	Korolev Simen	Misakova Marina
51.	Vladimer	15/2	-"-	Ivanskuk Petr	Harskakova Tonja
52.					

Repatriation list of Soviet children born in the Langstranda prison camp in 1944–45. Yuri is number 19.

2

YURI: THE BOY WITH THE "UNDESIRABLE BACKGROUND"

In connection with my research into vocational education and the labor market—the focus of my career since the 1970s—I was back in St. Petersburg in September of 2006, taking with me a group of students for an event at the Herzen State Pedagogical University. The university sits by the Moyka River, only several hundred feet from the Stroganov Palace and the shop where I had initially met Yuri's son Mikhail. Almost a year had gone by since I sent him the letter including the Digital Archives survey of Soviet prisoners returned in 1945, and I had not heard from the Salnikov family since then. Later, I found out that Yuri and his wife Natalya are not letter-writers, nor do they use the internet; Mikhail sees to all their correspondence.

Being close by, I decided to visit the giftshop again after the meeting at the university. I was curious: had they received my letter?

When I got to the shop, two women were assisting the customers. I asked for Mikhail Salnikov, explaining that I had met him in the shop a year ago and that I had sent him some information about his father. One of the women embraced me with tears in her eyes: it was Yuri's wife Natalya. Tall and elegant, and competent in English as a result of her studies in librarianship, Natalya overwhelmed me with hugs and said again and again how grateful they were for the proof I had found about Yuri's birth. She picked up her phone and called her husband to tell him I was in St. Petersburg. Since I had the next day off before returning to Oslo, we agreed they would pick me up at my bed and breakfast.

And so I finally met Yuri. A tall, slim man, he wears a black sailor's cap, his trademark, and has a white beard and friendly eyes. He speaks only Russian, but Natalya translated ably, and as our conversation proceeded, I began to comprehend the enormous significance this information had for Yuri and his family, who had lived with silence and lies for so many years.

The first lie was in the most basic document collected by all government bureaucracies: Yuri's birth certificate was issued in Vladivostok, where Galina and Fedor had registered him in 1947. Galina gave birth to their second son, Leonid, at a hospital in Vladivostok on March 18, 1947, three days after she and Fedor had married. They registered Yuri's date of birth as the same as his brother.

Galina and Fedor with their two sons, the supposed "twins" Yuri and Leonid, in Vladivostok in 1950. (Photo courtesy Yuri Salnikov.)

For many of his early years, Yuri believed he was his brother's twin. It was only in June 1958, when he was living with his parents and brother in Klaipeda, Lithuania's major seaport on the Baltic, that he learned that the story was false. Yuri often visited his Korolenko grandparents in St. Petersburg (known as Leningrad at the time), and was especially close to his grandmother, Anastasia. It was while visiting her that Yuri learned his mother, Galina, had come from Norway in 1945 with him in her arms.

The Secret of the Scissors

With obvious emotion, Yuri told us that it was his mother's brother, Mikhail, who revealed this secret. Uncle Mikhail was twenty-nine years old, a pilot and aerial photographer who worked all over the Soviet Union. His wife Raisa was a mathematics teacher at the prestigious Kadett Academy in Leningrad. There was a housing shortage, and Mikhail and Raisa lived with his parents in the family's minuscule apartment by the Gribordova Canal, where they had lived since before World War II.

During this visit, Yuri picked up a pair of scissors lying on the kitchen table. Looking closely, he made out the name "Solingen" engraved in the metal, in Latin letters rather than Cyrillic. He asked his uncle: "What is written on these scissors? What does Solingen mean? Where do these scissors come from?"

Mikhail answered, "Your mother brought these scissors with her from Norway. When she came back to Leningrad in 1945, she had you in her arms, the scissors, and many cans of fish. She had been a prisoner in Norway for three years. You were born in Norway."

Mikhail continued, "Your mother was visiting our Aunt Klaudia and Uncle Ivan in Gzhatsk when the Germans invaded the Soviet Union in 1941. She was seventeen years old when the Nazis abducted her."

Yuri was stunned at the news. His parents had never uttered a word about their war experiences in Norway, and would refuse to speak of it all their lives. Yuri did not know where or what Solingen was. But these scissors now gave him certainty about something he had sensed but never truly known.

As he later learned, the scissors were made in the Heinrich Brothers factory in Solingen, a town in North Rhineland/Westphalia in Germany. The region is called Bergische Land, and is regarded as the birthplace of German industrialization in the nineteenth century. During World War II, Belgian prisoners of war kept production going making war materials, not scissors. Today the factory has been converted into the industry museum called Gesenkschmiede Hendrichs.

We cannot know with certainty how the scissors came to Norway. They may have come with German soldiers as a personal belonging or have been commercially imported to Norway. But what is certain is that the scissors arrived in Leningrad with Yuri's mother Galina in August 1945.

It was also certain that his father, Fedor, was not with Galina and Yuri when they turned up at the family apartment. Yuri began asking questions. Where in Norway was his birthplace? Why were his parents in Norway in the middle of the war, and why were they not together when they arrived back in Russia? And perhaps most mysterious: why had it taken sixty years for Yuri to learn where he was born?

Some days after my visit to the giftshop, Natalya and Yuri came to pick me up at Rand House bed and breakfast on Bolshoya Morskaya, not far from the famous Hotel Astoria and the grand St. Isaac's Cathedral. Our conversation that day started a journey backward in time, one that explained to me a great deal about life in postwar Soviet Union, and why it had been so difficult to find the truth about his family's history.

They told me the story of how they met in 1968, on the steps of the fashionable Grand Hotel Europa on Nevsky Prospect. The building is one of St. Petersburg's architectural jewels, adorned with stained glass and a beautiful atrium. In the 1960s, it was a popular meeting place for young people, and on a chilly February day, Yuri was there with his cousin Andre Bliok. Both were students at the Ilya Repin Leningrad Institute for Painting, Sculpture, and Architecture. Yuri was twenty-four, Natalya nineteen and studying to become a librarian.

Natalya was there with a girlfriend. She was ascending the great marble steps and he was on his way down when, as they put it, an electric current passed between them.

However, they faced a difficult time. Natalya had just lost her mother and lived with her father, Peter Nikitich Romanov, and her brother Valery, at Gagarinskaya 3, in the middle of the city. Her father was a KGB general and regiment commissar in St. Petersburg. He was shocked by his daughter's relationship with Yuri, whom he considered to come from an undesirable family with a dangerous background. He was opposed to their relationship from the start. Yuri recalls being "interrogated" by the general about where he was born, where he grew up, who his parents were. When Yuri asked about what his parents had to do with his relationship with Natalya, the answer was clear: "Your parents' past can affect my daughter's future."

Natalya and Yuri defied the KGB general and married in Leningrad on March 13, 1969. Their son Mikhail was born in 1975.

Natalya and Yuri's wedding in Leningrad on March 13, 1969. (Photo courtesy of Yuri Salnikov.)

12 Gribordova Street

That morning, the first place they brought me to was the building on the Gribordova Canal, where Galina Korolenko was born. Yuri's grandmother, Anastasia Yakolevna Korolenko, and grandfather, Ivan

Nicolevich Korolenko, had lived here when Galina and her infant son Yuri returned from Norway.

Yuri clearly remembers being five years old (actually seven, but we will understand the confusion better a bit further on) and visiting the bombed-out ground-floor apartment at the back of the building. He recalls how crowded it was: everyone lived, slept, and ate in one 150 square foot room. The building was under reconstruction for many years. But the Korolenko family was happy to have survived the blockade of Leningrad and the German war machine's constant attacks. One can still see the effects of the hail of bombs, bullets, and shrapnel that hit Leningrad. The apartment at 12 Gribordova was hit again and again. Of the four-floor-high building, only a skeleton was left standing in 1945. But the family fixed up the ground-floor apartment and continued to live there.

Until Yuri received our initial information and began asking questions, however, he had no idea that his first acquaintance with the building had been in 1945, on Galina's return to Leningrad, when she suddenly stood before Anastasia with him in her arms. The canned fish she brought with her were much appreciated in Leningrad, a hungry city deeply marked by war and the years with hardly any food. The time of rationing cards was not yet over, and would not be for a long time to come.

Today, the building has been restored but it bears signs of wear and tear. The narrow room that Galina and Yuri came home to in 1945, and which Yuri remembers with a glow of love and nostalgia, is now a barbershop and tattoo parlor. Barbershop Headbusters was established there in 2012. Three young men wash and cut hair, shave using the traditional method with a razor, and also do tattoos for their youthful clientele. When I revisited the building in 2015, long after many of the questions posed in the writing of this book were answered, I watched as Yuri told the proprietors and their customers the room's story, the room where his grandmother and grandfather lived until their death and where he often visited and lived during his student years. He tells his war history to a completely new generation; the hairdressers sat quietly, listening with respect, their eyes lighting up with amazement.

Chapter 2

A Family Under Suspicion

Yuri rarely talks about the men in the family, be it his grandfather Valentin or even his own father, Fedor, who himself spoke little about his past or that of his family. Yuri remembers Fedor receiving the message of his own father's death in 1956. He remembers his father's tears. But the rest is a blank. There is no mention of Fedor's father in the Russian records, and what happened to that side of his family is another mystery. As Yuri later found out during his own research, he was listed with his mother's surname Korolenko in the Leningrad registry paper of 1945; no father was listed on the certificate.

The women are the focal points of his stories. He speaks warmly and at length about his grandmother as we stand facing the stalwart brick building, where he spent much of his childhood and youth with her. But she almost never spoke to him about the war years and told Yuri little about his parents and his background.

Silence and a kind of willful amnesia were the safest postwar strategies for Soviet citizens, something that also characterized Norway in the Cold War years. The Nobel Prize winner Svetlana Alexievich writes that people believed that everything would change after the war, and that Stalin would come to trust his people. But this did not happen. She says, "After the Victory everybody became silent. Silent and afraid, as before the war." Vladimir Putin has said, "My grandfather kept pretty quiet about his past life. My parents didn't talk much about the past, either. People generally didn't, back then."

For his part, Yuri says that Joseph Stalin was both "a wolf and a fox," both brutal and cunning, and that the way he ran the Soviet Union fundamentally affected relationships between people in the postwar years. People kept a lid on the past, a lid that concealed many secrets. The spirit of the times was marked by the fear that whispers of the past might devastate the future. It later turned out that Galina had kept some documents from Norway and from her journey home, but the family kept those years secret, including the birth of their first child in that country.

Galina and Yuri did not stay long in Leningrad, but instead set out across the continent to find Fedor who, as we will see later on, had been sent to Vladivostok to fight the Japanese rather than accompanying his wife and son to Leningrad. Documents found by Yuri in the city's archives in 2010 indicate that they may have left on March 6, 1946. They boarded a train for Moscow, then took the Trans-Siberian line from the Yaroslav Station in the center of the capital, all the way to Vladivostok. This railway traverses the entirety of this huge country, from Moscow in the west through Siberia to Vladivostok on the Pacific Ocean, a distance of 9,289 kilometers and many different continental time zones. Galina must have spent nine days on this long journey in the early spring of 1946, seeing millions of spruce and birch trees coming into leaf as she came closer and closer to the father of her child, Fedor.

Fortunately for the family, the Japanese capitulated on September 2, 1945. With World War II over at last, Fedor found employment in a shipyard. He had by now retaken his birth name of Salnikov. Galina and Fedor married and had another son in Vladivostok, and on March 27, 1947, Yuri was registered there under the last name of Salnikov. The family lived in Vladivostok for five years.

But the Soviet Union's tortuous political history and culture of secrecy and blame once again intervened. Yuri's understanding is that Fedor lost his job in Vladivostok when the shipyard was taken over by the military. There had been an accident at the yard and one person died. An inquiry took place, during which it was discovered that Fedor had been a prisoner of war. Accused of being a saboteur, he was forced to quit. The authorities decided where people could settle, and the family was not granted permission to live in Leningrad, despite having relatives there.

A New Life in the Soviet Republic of Lithuania

Despite these developments, Fedor had friends in the relevant ministry and got help in seeking employment at a new shipyard on the other side of the continent, in the port city of Klaipeda.

This area of the world has a brutal and complex history. It had traditionally been populated by Huguenots, German and Polish Catholics, Lithuanians, Russians, and many others. For hundreds of years, while it was part of the East-Prussian realm, Klaipeda was called Memel, and the official language was German, but many languages could be heard in the streets of these cities. After World War I, the city became part of Lithuania and was named Klaipeda. In 1938, Hitler demanded that the city be returned. It became part of Germany once again—and the marketplace renamed Adolf Hitler-Platz—in the following year.

The war years devastated the city, including fierce house-to-house fighting during the last days of January 1945. When the Red Army occupied the city on January 28, the city was almost deserted. The German population had fled to avoid the Russians. The inhabitants present when the Red Army arrived were among the approximately twelve million ethnic Germans who had fled or been expelled from Eastern and Central Europe as the fighting came to an end. This expulsion—in the words of historian Neal Acherson, "a gigantic act of ethnic cleansing, as we would now call it"—had the approval of the Western Allies, who saw ethnic minorities as threats to national stability. In 1944, Winston Churchill told the House of Commons that huge population transfers would be necessary after the war ended, including

> the total expulsion of the Germans...from the area to be acquired by Poland in the west and the north. For expulsion is the method which, so far as we have been able to see, will be the most satisfactory and lasting. There will be no mixture of populations to cause endless trouble, as has been the case in Alsace-Lorraine.

In the final settlements of World War II, Klaipeda was ceded from Germany to the Soviet Union and became part of the Soviet Republic of Lithuania. A new epoch began. The Soviets made this ice-free port on the Baltic a center of shipbuilding and repair for fishing and merchant fleets, with both new and refurbished historic shipyards beginning in the early 1950s. This was where Fedor Salnikov began work as an electrical engineer in 1951, and the family moved from Vladivostok to Klaipeda.

They were allotted an apartment in the center of the city, in Montas Street. Yuri's father had no documents certifying his vocational education, owing to his time spent as a prisoner of war. But he was good at his work and his fellow workers called him "Doctor." Yuri believes his father learned a lot during his time as a slave laborer in Norway. In the Russian archives, he is listed as an electrician. Yuri's second brother Vladimir was born on January 3, 1951, in Klaipeda. Their parents stayed in Klaipeda until their deaths, Fedor lived until 1987, Galina until 1992.

3

AN ARTIST'S LIFE

As he grew older, Yuri originally received a technical education, studying shipbuilding at Klaipeda Kavaliskosh Luizes Gymnasium, a stately building that had been the Gestapo headquarters during the war. To this day, he refers to himself as a "master craftsman."

From an early age he liked to draw, and his grandmother gave him his first drawing and writing materials. His cousin and friend Andre Bliok, today an eminent Russian painter, had entered the Ilya Repin Leningrad Institute for Painting, Sculpture, and Architecture in 1965, and suggested that Yuri apply. Yuri started his art education there in 1966. The institute was founded in 1757 as the St. Petersburg Academy of Art, and has changed its name many times. Since 1991 it has once again been called St. Petersburg Institute for Painting, Sculpture, and Architecture.

During our first meeting in 2006, Yuri and Natalya brought me to this majestic building by the Neva River, where we joined the city's inhabitants in strolling sociably and admiring the architecture and the art. We continued to Kamennostrovsky Prospect 1/3-35, an impressive building in the art nouveau style, built at the beginning of the twentieth century. The building is close to the Peter and Paul Fortress, where Feodor Dostoyevsky was imprisoned while awaiting his execution in 1849. (We can thank Czar Nicolas I that this did not happen. Instead, Dostoyevsky was sent to Siberia but returned to St. Petersburg and created literature marked by his years in Siberia; his texts will probably never cease to touch us, his readers.)

Yuri and Natalya have an apartment there. Yet his career was not easy in his early years, not least because it was difficult to become a member of the Artists' Union of the USSR. But in 1983 a winning bid for a large work in Kyiv changed his life. His sculpture, created for the city of Kyiv's 1,500-year anniversary, occupied him for two years, between 1983 and 1985. Yuri says the monument was destroyed in 2015, as were other examples of his monumental works around the former Soviet Union.

The Kyiv sculpture opened the doors for Yuri, and since then he has worked on projects from St. Petersburg to Kazakhstan. One of his copperplate prints is exhibited in the museum-ship *Aurora,* a stone's throw from their St. Petersburg apartment.

The Treasure Trove of Photos

The following day, we continued our journey to the suburb of Sestroretsk, outside St. Petersburg. Yuri and Natalya have built a *dacha* there, a labor of love and a work of art, that Yuri designed and in part built himself. His traditional art education is apparent in the importance he has placed on solid craftsmanship, including elegant garden outbuildings. His workshop is filled with sketches and engravings, primarily copperplate engravings; his tools, diamond needles, loupes, and sharpening stones play a very important role in this process.

We sat down to a beautiful table with all kinds of Russian delicacies: caviar, blinis, red beet and potato salad, mushrooms, sliced smoked ham, and tongue. There was wine and vodka on the table. After the meal, Yuri brought out an old wallet and photographs. They told me they found the photographs and the wallet after his mother's death in 1992.

Fish-skin wallet containing photos of Yuri's parents, some of which were taken in Bodø in 1945. (Photo: Liv Mjelde.)

The wallet, fashioned from fish-skin leather, is decorated on one side with a sailing ship, and on the other with a high mountain, a shining sun, and a lighthouse. An inscription on it reads *Bodø194-*. The last number is gone. But the name Bodø—a medium-sized town in the north of Norway—was well known to me.

There were many pictures in the wallet. The backgrounds of some photos show mountains and leaf-bearing trees, and in all of them the people are dressed lightly in civilian clothes. Spring and liberation had come to the north. One shows a large group, mostly women, standing in front of barracks, four of them carrying infants. Galina is in the photo, but there is no child with her. In another dated May 1, 1945, Galina and Fedor stand side by side, staring apprehensively at the camera.

The back of a photo of Fedor alone bears a handwritten note: "To Galina. If we do not meet again, let this picture of Fedor's face remain in Galina's memory." His words show the uncertainty they must have felt about their future after their return to the Soviet Union.

They were going home and were registered on a list as the mother and father of five-month-old Yuri. But whether they would be living together seemed uncertain. Perhaps Fedor's complicated Kulak background and the fact that he had been taken prisoner during a military operation made him change his name. It is likely that all prisoners of war knew Stalin's famous Order No. 227, "Not one step back!" under which anyone who retreated without authorization would be dealt with as a traitor to the motherland.

The wallet and photographs were potential clues to the mystery of Yuri's birthplace. It might have been Bodø and was perhaps linked to a fish processing factory, probably associated with the abundant cod fishery around the Lofoten Islands. Because of the cans of fish that Galina had brought to Leningrad in 1945, we suspected that his birthplace was somehow related to the fishing industry.

I returned to Oslo with new questions, new data, and a stack of photos Yuri had given me.

The Truth of Yuri's Birthplace

As it happened, soon after my return to Norway, I was scheduled to carry out a routine academic task that would take me north from Oslo. A teacher who worked at the university college in Bodø was to defend her doctoral dissertation at the University of Tromsø, which is about 500 kilometers further north. I was appointed as "opponent"—the Scandinavian equivalent of an external examiner—in the candidate's defense of her doctoral thesis.

When I met another colleague from the university for breakfast, I showed her the photos. My colleague Elisabeth Nilsen was born in Saltstraumen on the outskirts of Bodø. She had lived in the area near Bodø all her life and was a member of the city government for many years. When I showed her the photos, she was flabbergasted. She was familiar with the horror stories about the treatment of Soviet male prisoners of war in Nordland, who had been set to build roads, the airport, the railway, and various defense installations. But she had never heard stories of Soviet women held as prisoners of war in Nordland during the occupation.

Elizabeth started looking into the matter and helped me trace people with a special interest in wartime history. Two more years would pass before Yuri had evidence of his birthplace.

Thanks to the Red Cross records from Langstranda that the Bodø-based historian and museum director Knut Støre had conserved, we found Galina, Fedor, and Yuri's names on the 1945 lists of prisoners of war, and of who had been forced laborers at the fish factory Frostfilet A/S at Langstranda outside Bodø. Two more years would pass before he had evidence of his birthplace. In 2008, thanks to the records held by Knut, he received proof that he had been born in a prison camp in northern Norway during the final phase of World War II. This was the secret his parents had guarded throughout their lives and which they took with them to the grave.

The vice-mayor of Bodø, Kirsten Hasvoll, was very interested in this new information about the fish factory and Soviet women laboring there during WWII. She had been born in Hungary, to Jewish parents, and became engrossed in the mystery. In 2008, the mayor sent an invitation to Yuri and Natalya, as well as to my husband and me, and the four of us visited Bodø in September of that year. We gave a seminar at the university college, describing the coincidences that had brought us to Bodø. For five days we were Bodø's guests of honor, and we were taken to visit the factory buildings of Frostfilet A/S, where Yuri's parents had lived and worked while prisoners of war. We were standing on the ground where Yuri had been born. He was able to see and feel his motherland, over six decades after he left it.

The question of Yuri's actual birthplace was now definitively solved. But large gaps remained in the stories of his parents, and whole new histories began to emerge of others—prisoners of war and Norwegian citizens—who had labored in the northern fish factories during WWII.

Yuri and Natalya Salnikov with the writer Dag Skogheim and historian Marianne Neerland Soleim in front of the war monument at Falstad in September 2008. (Photo: Liv Mjelde.)

4

FEDOR: A GRAND ALLIANCE AND A GREAT BETRAYAL

One of the results of Yuri finally learning where he had been born is that he started to investigate his parents' history in the Soviet Union. He eventually tracked down a number of documents, including one showing Galina's arrival in Leningrad in August 1945, where she registered him without the name of the father.

He also began to join up the dots between what he learned and the little his parents and other relatives had told him. While his father had talked about his experiences as a soldier in the Red Army, including his capture, he never talked about his experiences as a prisoner of war in Norway.

According to government archives, Fedor Vasilievich Salnikov was born on October 16, 1918, in Novosibirskaya *Oblast* (district), in the geographic center of Russia. Fedor had ancestors among the Ukrainian Kulaks who were sent to Siberia from the Zhytomyr Oblast. His parents are listed as having lived in Siberia from the 1930s.

But the Russian archives and the Bodø lists give contradictory information on this subject. The Bodø list gives his last name as Savin and his birthplace as Zhytomyr in western Ukraine. Yuri does not know exactly what the truth might have been, though he believes his father received his training as an electrician at the technical college in

Zhytomyr. It is possible that Fedor was born there and moved with his parents to Novosibirsk in the 1930s. His mother's name, Salnikov, does not appear in the Bodø lists, while in the Soviet archives his mother, Matryona Afansievna Salnikova, is the only person listed as his next-of-kin, with no mention of a father besides the patronymic Vasilievich (son of Vasily). It is possible that Fedor was afraid to mention his father's name.

Official records lose track of Fedor until August 1939, when he turns up at a pivotal moment in history.

Fedor Savin Salnikov, aged 27 on May 1, 1945. (Photo: Fedor Salnikov.)

The Great Patriotic War Begins

On August 23, 1939, the Soviet Union and Germany signed a non-aggression pact with a secret clause establishing Soviet and German spheres of influence in Eastern Europe. The Molotov–Ribbentrop Pact recognized Estonia, Latvia, and Bessarabia (now split between Moldova and Ukraine) as falling within the Soviet sphere of influence, while Poland was divided between the two powers along the line of the Narev, Vistula, and San Rivers. The following week, Germany invaded Poland, leading to a declaration of war by France and Great Britain on September 3.

A month later, German and Soviet soldiers stood side by side during a celebratory parade in the streets of Brest-Litovsk (now Brest, in Belarus) on September 22. Under the pact, the territory around Brest-Litovsk, along with 52 percent of occupied Poland, was given over to Soviet occupation.

Yuri remembers his father saying that he was one of the Soviet soldiers taking part in the parade. Records from the memorial archives of the Russian Ministry of Defense confirm that Fedor was called up for military service on August 13, 1939; oddly, the place of recruitment is given as south Kazakhstan. How and why he found himself assigned to parade duty in Brest-Litovsk five weeks later is a mystery, but military machines have their own logic.

The agreement lasted for a year and ten months, until Germany launched Operation Barbarossa and began its invasion of the Soviet Union.

The German assault began on Sunday, June 22, the longest day of the year, on which the sun shines at midnight in the far north. Inhabitants across the western Soviet Union were busy preparing for the mid-summer festivities when nearly four million men in motorized vehicles and on horseback poured across the length of the Soviet border from the south to the far north. Foreign Minister Molotov was visited by the German ambassador to USSR at 5:30 a.m. on June 22. Ambassador von Schulenburg informed him that Germany had decided to attack because of the concentration of Soviet troops on the border. The Soviet population was informed by Molotov via radio transmission the same day.

In the days that followed, people began to register for service. Among the thousands who wanted to join in the fight were Galina's father in Leningrad and her uncle Ivan in Gzhatsk, a town to the East of Moscow. Women as well as men stood in long lines in front of the recruitment offices all over the Soviet Union. The Soviet population's active participation in civilian and military resistance and production was a genuine grassroots response to the German invasion.

All over the Soviet Union, people heard Stalin's radio address on July 3, which opened with the words: "Comrades, citizens, brothers and sisters, fighters of our army and navy! I am speaking to you, my friends!" It was his first speech after the German invasion. The Russian-born journalist Alexander Werth described it as an unusual performance, not least the opening line: Stalin was not known to address his people in such familiar terms. He began by saying that the Nazi invasion continued despite the Red Army's valiant defense and that Lithuania and Latvia, large parts of Belarus, and the western part of the Ukraine were already occupied by the Germans.

The Soviet Union was, by any reasonable measure, badly prepared for war, as intelligence failures were compounded by a combination of the long shadow of the Great Terror, the strategic culture of the Soviet Union, and its lackluster military reforms.

Zhytomyr was occupied by the Germans on July 9, 1941, and became Heinrich Himmler's Ukrainian headquarters, as well as the laboratory for the Nazi Aryan settlement plans. A large Jewish center with a mostly Hasidic population, the town had three large synagogues and forty-six small Talmudic schools. The Jewish communities in the district were quickly eliminated and on July 25, Himmler ordered that all of Ukraine's Jewish villages and ghettos be reduced to ruins. Thousands upon thousands of Jewish men, women, and children were brutally murdered by stationary and mobile SS-units and their local Ukrainian collaborators. Himmler also insisted that the Slavic Ukrainian population not be spared: the number of Slavs was to be reduced to a minimum to make room for the new Aryan race, which included Norwegians. The Baltic States, Poland, and the Ukraine were the geographic centers of this barbaric policy of mass extermination of Jews. Plans for the Pan-Germanic colonization transformed both nature and culture as violence, terror, and murder became the order of the day. Jews and Communists were to be shot immediately. Slavic *Untermenschen* were to be driven out or destroyed.

Captured at the Battle of Kyiv

On September 19, the German troops entered Kyiv. The commanding officer went immediately to the legendary Kyiv-Pechersk Lavra and let the triumphal church-bells ring out across the district. The cloister buildings were situated on the highest point in Kyiv and were surrounded by high walls, making it an easily defensible position for the Germans.

The repercussions of the German victory were immediate and horrific. It was barely ten days later that Babi Yar, on the outskirts of Kyiv, became the site of one of the biggest massacres of Jews during World War II. Over the course of two days, an estimated 33,771 Jews were marched to the Babi Yar ravine, ordered to remove their clothing, and shot in small groups. Only twenty-nine people are known to have survived. The Jewish population of Kyiv was decimated in a matter of forty-eight hours. Soviet marine prisoners from ships on the Dnieper River were marched through the city to Babi Yar, where their final job was to throw dirt over the corpses. Then they themselves were shot and thrown into the ravine. Babi Yar continued to be used by German troops as an execution site for Jews and other victims of Nazi persecution, including Roma and Soviet prisoners of war, until 1943.

Soviet POWs forced to cover a mass grave after the Babi Yar massacre, October 1, 1941. (Photo: Johannes Hähle via Wikimedia Commons.)

Records that Yuri found in Russian military archives state that Assistant Platoon Sergeant Fedor Salnikov was taken prisoner during the large pincer maneuver of the Battle of Kyiv in 1941, which had resulted in over half a million Soviet soldiers being surrounded. He was at that time in the Eighty-First Detachment of the Motorized Engineer Battalion of the Nineteenth Corps. The records state that Fedor was captured on September 24, near Baryshivka in Kieskaya Oblast, twenty to thirty kilometers southeast of central Kyiv, and that he was reported missing that same day.

However, Yuri says his father told him a different story: that he was taken prisoner in the small village of Brovari, around twenty kilometers north of Kyiv, where he had been working as an electrician at the local electrical station. He told Yuri that was where his battalion surrendered.

Both claims may be true. Fedor may have been taken prisoner in Brovari and been registered in Baryshivka, or the other way around. The situation was chaotic. A total of 616,000 soldiers surrendered during the Battle of Kyiv, with most of them becoming prisoners of war. Nazi Germany was known for its bureaucratic precision and thorough registration practices, but taking down data on the millions of Soviet citizens who were captured in these battles in 1941 was a demanding task. The Germans had also been indoctrinated to regard these people as inferior human beings that they would prefer to eradicate from the surface of the earth. Why bother registering them?

The prisoners' trials and suffering had barely begun. Fedor Salnikov, along with hundreds of thousands of other prisoners of war, was marched westward to reception centers which were built in occupied Soviet territories, as well as in Germany and other countries. There was no rest during the journey, and Fedor told Yuri that they slept in the open.

The prisoners were given no food, forcing them to strip bark from trees and eat it in desperation. They used sticks to try to make fires. They were not dressed for the cold and slept close together to keep warm, yet every morning there were still dead bodies among them, who were simply left behind when the order came to keep walking. The wounded could expect no help, and prisoners who lagged or broke down during the march were shot. Such brutal conditions led to mass deaths. Soviet prisoners of war were cordoned off in a field behind barbed-wire fences and left to the elements without any protection of any kind. Food was sporadically thrown into the camp, and sanitation was catastrophic. They died like flies. The German authorities regarded the Soviet prisoners of war as undesirable elements, the feeding of whom was a waste of resources.

Many prisoners nevertheless survived long enough to reach a prison camp, and Yuri's father was one of them. A change in Nazi policy, spurred on by the need for labor power, may have increased his chances of survival.

As will be discussed in more depth later in the book, the occupying Germans began to modify their policies in 1941. Germany and Norway needed workers for their factories and farms. Nazi leadership began to think of prisoners of war as a potential pool of labor. Skilled laborers were a desirable commodity in the German Reich and within the concentration camp system. If one were able to practice the skills that Germany needed, one might avoid the gas chamber. If one were a seamstress or a tailor, one's hands could be used to sew uniforms; shoemakers were needed to produce shoes and boots for the Wehrmacht. If one had an education in graphic arts, that knowledge could be used to produce counterfeit British pound notes, something prisoners in Sachsenhausen concentration camp specialized in. Carpenters, masons, welders, and concrete workers were important to the construction industries in the Third Reich, while electrical and refrigeration specialists were important to the frozen fish industry. Fedor's background as an electrician may have saved his life.

How did he get from the battlefields of Ukraine to Norway? Transportation records reveal that most of the Soviet prisoners of war were sent through the port city of Stettin (now Szczecin in Poland), which was a central base for trade to Scandinavia during the war, and the site of massive forced-labor plants. If this was Fedor's route, he may have been carried by the SS *Donau*. A freighter that came to be known as "the slave ship," the *Donau* was requisitioned by the German navy in 1940, and was used to transport starving prisoners of war to forced-labor camps in Norway and to transport Norwegian Jews and other prisoners back to Germany and occupied Poland. Another freighter, the *Monte Rosa*—later famous in the United Kingdom under the name *Empire Windrush*—was used for the same purpose.

Four transfers from Germany went directly by boat to northern Norway in 1941 with a total of 3,253 prisoners. Fedor may have been one of these prisoners, but we cannot know for sure. Nor can we do more than speculate about how he met Galina, who enters into the story under very different circumstances.

5

GALINA: A CITY STARVED, A GIRL ABDUCTED

Years after our first meetings with Yuri, my husband and I found ourselves in a well-used Chevrolet Cruze on the road to Gagarin. There we planned to look for the place where Galina had disappeared, and to see the War Museum in Gagarin. Formerly called Gzhatsk, and renamed after the first cosmonaut Yuri Gagarin, the town sits east of Leningrad roughly halfway between Smolensk and Moscow on the Gzhatsk River.

Our chauffeur was a fast driver who had a telescreen blaring soap operas in front of him throughout our journey, along with two mobile phones ringing sporadically. We also had a guide who frequently exclaimed "*poehali*" ("let's go"). He eventually explained that Russians say *poehali* when they have had a few shots of vodka, echoing Yuri Gagarin's muttered exclamation from the spaceship *Vostok 1* on April 12, 1961, indicating that he was ready for lift-off and the first journey into space.

We passed Borodino on our way, the place where Napoleon lost 300,000 men, who starved and froze to death in the Russian winter. We began to look for Artemki, where Galina Korolenko's life was changed. Turning after a sign marked *АРТЁМКИ*, we drove down a small side road, where we saw the remains of an agricultural collective.

An older man gave us directions and, further down a gravel road, we found the figure of a soldier in shiny steel standing in a memorial grove surrounded by trees. This figure marks the site of the great Battle of Artemki of October 9, 1941. A small plaque carries the inscription:

> *"Your destiny, Siberian fidelity to your motherland, is eternal in our hearts. From the residents of the town of Rubtsovsk, Altai Region, May 1971."*

Another plaque carries the inscription:

> *"Here in October 1941, soldiers, sergeants and officers of the 154th Howitzer Artillery Regiment and the Thirty-Second Red-Banner Rifle Division fought to their death defending Moscow. From fraternal soldiers, May 1976."*

Fresh flowers placed by the statue made it clear that the fallen soldiers have not been forgotten. The village was conquered and occupied by the Germans on October 9, 1941; the occupation lasted until March 6, 1943, in Artemki as well as in Gagarin.

After a thirty-minute drive from Artemki, we finally arrived in Gargarin. A commuter town of around 30,000 to 40,000 inhabitants, there is a bullet-train to Moscow and new apartments are being built everywhere. As the hometown of the first cosmonaut, it is also a tourist attraction. The history museum holds a large exhibit of paintings dedicated to Yuri Gagarin, as well as a substantial exhibition about the plight of the town during World War II. A large brick building in the midst of town, it was once a school Gagarin attended, and was one of the few structures still left standing when the Germans were forced to withdraw.

There we met the second wife of Yuri's uncle Mikhail, who took us to the Korolenko house in central Gargarin. With his help, we picked up more of Galina's story, so far as the family and limited documentary evidence can tell us.

Days before the German invasion, sixteen-year-old-Galina said goodbye to her parents in Leningrad (as St. Petersburg was then known) and went to visit her Aunt Klaudia and Uncle Ivan. It was during her summer vacation, which lasted for three months from June

1 to September 1. Klaudia and Ivan had three sons and lived in a little timber-frame house in the middle of town. The house was small but there was always room for relatives, and family ties were close. Galina had often accompanied her parents there on visits, but it was common practice for city children to travel alone to their relatives in the country

That goodbye was the last time that Galina's parents would see her until she showed up at 12 Gribordova Street in 1945, with the infant Yuri in her arms.

Yuri with his mother Galina Korolenko after their arrival home in Leningrad in 1945. (Photo courtesy Yuri Salnikov.)

Leningrad Besieged (1941–44)

The events of the war severed all contact between Leningrad and the rest of the Soviet Union during the long siege, which lasted from September 1941 to January 1944. On September 8, 1941, the German forces were just sixteen kilometers from the city and the Wehrmacht's High Command announced: "The iron ring around Leningrad has been closed."

A secret directive written by Hitler indicated that the plan was to "erase the city of Petersburg from the face of the earth," essentially by starving the population to death. From September 1941 until the end of May 1942, nearly one million people died of hunger, exhaustion, and disease. There was no food for long periods during the blockade, and it was eventually rationed to 175 grams of sawdust-bread per day.

Like many Soviet families, Galina's parents kept their memories of this terrible period alive in countless stories. Galina's mother Anastasia made soup from boot leather. Everything went into the family soup. Sometimes there was carpenter's glue that would be mixed with tree bark and grass—if and when they could find these ingredients. Heating was another serious problem. The cold was intense in Leningrad in January and February, and there was no wood. People froze to death and collapsed in the streets.

Galina's father, Valentin, worked as a supervisor at a factory on the city's east side, not far from the Smolny Cathedral, which had been Lenin's headquarters during the Russian Revolution. Every day, Galina's brother, eleven-year-old Mikhail, walked the long road from the Gribordova Canal to the factory in hope of gathering some breadcrumbs. Valentin was responsible for distributing bread to the workers, and some crumbs were left after the bread was sliced. Mikhail put the crumbs he got from his father inside the lining of his jacket and smuggled them home for the evening's soup. The journey took two to three hours each way, and his mother Anastasia was always worried: would he get home in one piece? In Leningrad in 1942, children were beginning to disappear from the streets. Rumors swirled that children were being killed and eaten. Young flesh was attractive to the starving. Cannibalism was punishable by death, but desperation drove people to the previously unthinkable. It is said that the thighs from frozen cadavers were cut off and eaten.

There were periods when more than 30,000 people died of hunger every day. People became weak and vulnerable to infections. Insect bites were now life-threatening and there were, then as now, legions of insects in Leningrad, from mosquitoes to bedbugs to a huge spectrum of spiders. The city was built, under Peter the Great, on a bog where the River Neva meets the Baltic Sea. Insects thrive in these conditions and their bites can be deadly to the vulnerable. At some point during the siege, Anastasia's brother Pavel died from an insect bite; he was thirty years old. The family wrapped him up and pulled him on a sled through the city to one of the designated grave sites. This was a common sight during those years when every family was touched and lost someone near and dear.

The only way to get into the city during the siege was across Lake Ladoga. Between May and November this meant taking a boat to the small fishing village of Ladozhskoye Ozero. When the lake froze in the wintertime, the journey went across the thick ice. From this village, a forty-six-kilometer gravel road, known as The Road of Life, began to function as an access point in late November 1941. By that time the situation was desperate. Whatever food and goods entered the city came through this little opening in the blockade. Many people were evacuated back out along the same route. The opening expanded after the Soviet offensive in May 1942, and new possibilities presented themselves to Leningrad's starving population. For those who had survived the first terrible year, it now became possible to assuage the worst hunger. But the battles went on relentlessly, across both land and water.

It was not until January 27, 1944, that Leningrad was once again a free city. It is estimated that the 872-day siege, known ever after as The 900 Days, had cost the lives of one-third of the city's population. Leningrad's strong resistance against the Germans gave the city the distinction of being a so-called Hero City, an honorary title accorded twelve cities in the Soviet Union for the struggles waged by their people during World War II.

Today the blockade is a vivid presence in the consciousness of Leningrad's citizens. Everyone has a story to tell, and memories travel down from one generation to the next. The citizens know their history. The blockade is at the core of the Salnikovs' stories, as if embedded within the walls of their house. They come back again and again to the family's experiences of Leningrad during the war.

Of Galina's fate, the family knew next to nothing. At the same time, the story of the village where she had gone to visit her relatives was only too well known.

Abduction

As is vividly documented in the Gagarin Museum, German soldiers had occupied Gzhatsk for eighteen long months. Brutality and destruction were rampant. Hitler's Hunger Plan was thoroughly instituted against the local population as well as for prisoners from the whole region. The occupying army commandeered the region's meat supplies and confiscated food in the nearby villages. The town's church was turned into an abattoir. There was a prison camp for Soviet soldiers in the town. There, they were given fifty grams of bread and a cup of water per day. Civilians who tried to give them food were severely punished.

Opposition grew quickly, and the partisans gained strength. The battles between the occupiers and partisans were bloody and cost thousands of lives, with partisan groups killing 7,000 German soldiers in this area. Unknown numbers of partisans and their supporters were also killed. The Germans did everything in their power to prevent the partisans from receiving support in the villages around Gzhatsk. As a precaution, these settlements were burned to the ground. Men, women, and children were corralled into barns and incinerated. The town had 32,000 inhabitants at the beginning of the war. When the Nazis retreated in 1943, only 7,500 people remained. Six thousand citizens had been sent by train from Gzhatsk to unknown destinations, among them 600 children under the age of fourteen.

It was only then that Anastasia and Valentin learned that, at some time during June or July 1941, Galina had fled with her aunt, uncle, and three cousins from Gzhatsk to Artemki, where she was abducted in 1942. The German offensive against Moscow started on September 30, 1941, and Gzhatsk was at the center of these plans. On October 13, 1941, the Wehrmacht's Fourth Panzer Army established its headquarters in Gzhatsk. Galina, her aunt, and cousins tried to escape to Moscow, but the car broke down. By then, her uncle Ivan, who was forty-seven years old, was in the infantry, but had been hurt in a battle and was in hospital. Over the winter, the family sought refuge with a miller family who lived by the river, moving in with another family in Artemki in 1942.

Young girls from the Soviet Union were rounded up by the Germans at the local railroad station and taken in cattle cars to work in the industries of Germany and Poland. (Photo: Unknown.)

We learned more from Galina's cousin Sergei, in a telephone conversation from Moscow in 2015. He was seven years old when he witnessed the German soldiers going from house to house and seizing young people, both girls and boys. Galina and the others were taken to the railroad station in Gzhatsk, he said, and simply disappeared. No one was told why, or where they were going.

As with Fedor, we know almost nothing about what happened next to Galina, or exactly how she arrived in Norway. And the fact is that we may never know, since the "normal" channels of inquiry have so far led us nowhere. For example, there is no documentation on Fedor or Galina in the Arolsen Archives, located near Frankfurt, which assists family members and researchers in their attempts to trace the fate of Nazi victims. Nor is there any information in the National Archives of Norway or Arkiv Nordland (Archive Nordland County) in Bodø. The names of Fedor and Galina only resurface on official lists of repatriation from Narvik in 1945 and on the lists of those who worked at the fish factory, Frostfilet A/S, in the town of Bodø.

PART II

FROZEN FISH AND SLAVE LABOR

6

THE NORDIC COUNTRIES IN HITLER'S WAR

On November 30, 1939, my grandmother-in-law Muriel Chillingwood Colls Reid wrote in her diary in Vancouver, Canada:

> Today Russia bombed Finland. What is the matter with the world making every small nation tremble in their shoes. It seems that the day for small nations is petering out. These two grand bullies of Europe, Germany & Russia, will come to loggerheads sometime. It is all so terrible or has human nature got something to learn to be made over?

It was thus that the Winter War between Finland and the Soviet Union began. After heavy losses on both sides, hostilities ended with the Moscow Peace Treaty on March 13, 1940. This lasted until June 21, 1941, when the region erupted once again with the German invasion of the Soviet Union. The fighting on Finnish soil, which eventually led to Finland concluding an alliance with Germany, called the Continuation War, lasted until 1944.

Muriel's worry about "the small nations" was well-founded. Only six months later, on April 9, 1940, the war arrived in Denmark and

Norway with Germany's Operation Weserübung. Justified as a preemptive strike to prevent a French–British occupation of Norway (something France and Britain had publicly discussed, though as a response against possible German aggression), the intervention did not go as smoothly as Hitler expected.

The two Scandinavian countries had hoped their neutrality would be respected. Threatened with devastating bombing, Denmark capitulated in less than a day, but in doing so managed to negotiate considerable political independence. The Danish royal family remained in the country.

In Norway, despite the country's almost complete lack of preparation, the Wermacht met strong resistance, starting with the sinking of the German battle cruiser *Blücher* near Oslo by gunfire and pre-World

War I torpedoes from the aging Oscarsborg Fortress. This unexpected feat of arms delayed the taking of the capital long enough for the Norwegian royal family and key government figures to escape their planned capture by the German forces.

The best-known action on Norwegian soil, the Battle of Narvik, lasted from April 9 until June 8, and only ended when British, French, and Polish troops withdrew, leaving the Norwegian forces on their own against overwhelming odds. Norway finally signed a capitulation agreement on June 10, 1940, in Trondheim. By that time, King Haakon VII, Crown Prince Olav, and other members of the Norwegian royal family had been evacuated to the United Kingdom, where they embodied the country's refusal to accept the German takeover.

Sweden was the only country in the north that avoided direct conflict with Germany. As Norwegian joke about the Nazi attack on Scandinavia puts it, "Operation Weserübung took Norway within two months. Denmark was conquered in one day. Sweden was taken with a phone call." Sweden's cooperation with the Nazi regime would later become a highly controversial moment in its history. During the interwar period, a polite acceptance of Nazi Germany had developed among Sweden's bourgeois and aristocratic circles. Much of this owed to the strong fear of the Bolshevik threat. The nation entered into several binding agreements with Germany as early as June 18, 1940, when Luleå became a supply depot for the German forces. The Wehrmacht were gradually given access to Sweden's railroad and telecommunications networks and, to a certain degree, its territorial waters and air space. Over the next three years, an estimated 2,140,000 soldiers and 100,000 trainloads of weapons and equipment were sent through Sweden to the German army in North Norway. Sweden also loaned 500 train cars, state-owned and private, to aid the all-important transportation of iron ore to Germany. This collaboration was concealed from the Swedish people, with transports taking place under cover of night, and remains marginalized in the history books of both Sweden and Norway.

The border between the two nations did, however, provide a point of escape for more than 50,000 Norwegian refugees during the war, including many Jews. As we will see in later chapters, Norway's resistance movement also received weapons and other equipment via Sweden; by 1943, the time was ripe to start training Norwegians to serve in the liberation of their homeland.

7

TO FEED AN ARMY

Though in military terms the invasion of Norway seemed like a minor sideshow compared to the blitzkrieg that overran Belgium, France, and the Netherlands in the summer of 1940, the strategic importance of Norway's fishing industry to the German war effort cannot be underestimated. Iron ore is important to the military, but soldiers can't eat it; as both Napoleon and Frederick the Great are reputed to have said, "an army marches on its stomach."

In his book *A Writer at War,* Vasily Grossman refers to a large, oval can of fish found in an abandoned bunker as an example of "Norway's contribution" to the German officers at the siege of Stalingrad. Norwegian canned fish was regarded as a delicacy meant for the officer class at the front. Grossman recorded that the enlisted men's bunkers presented a very different sight: "Here one won't see empty chocolate boxes and unfinished sardines. There are only tins of pressed peas and chunks of bread as heavy as cast iron."

Along with frozen fish, the tinned version was also regarded as a delicacy by the German civilian population. In the years 1943–44, 50 percent of Germany's supply of fresh fish, and an astonishing 100 percent of Germany's canned fish, came from Norway. They were vital provisions both for the front and for the occupying German army in

Norway, which at the end of the war numbered more than 300,000 soldiers who needed to be fed daily.

At the end of the 1930s, Norway had Europe's largest fisheries, with Lofoten cod and herring from the Barents Sea. After the invasion of Norway, this came to be of great importance to provisioning the Wehrmacht and the wider German population.

Monroe Doktrine für Europa

The Germans had early on made extensive plans for the Norwegian fisheries within a *Grossraumwirtschaft,* an expansive European economic zone wherein the different regions of the German Reich would contribute what they were best suited to supply. The work of the German political thinker Carl Schmitt (1888–1985) was an inspiration for this kind of planning. Between the two wars, Schmitt was one of the preeminent legal and strategic minds in Germany. He admired the American empire and the strategies that animated it, the best expression of which he considered to be the Monroe Doctrine of 1823, spearheaded by President James Monroe. In the Monroe Doctrine, the United States declared that the European powers must not interfere within its spheres of interest in North and South America. Within this zone, the US would decide which actions could be deemed peaceful, and which were interventions.

Adolf Hitler dreamt of creating a Monroe Doctrine for Europe and *Lebensraum für die Arische Rassen* (living space for the Aryan race). In his book *Mein Kampf,* written in prison in the 1920s, Hitler had already envisioned the invasion of the Soviet Union. The inevitability of German expansionism mandated the extermination of the Slavic peoples, as well as the acquisition of land and raw materials. Both of the latter could be found in abundance in the East.

In July 1941, Hitler announced the coming creation of a so-called "Garden of Eden" for the Aryan race in Eastern Europe. The Third Reich considered the Soviet Union to be inhabited by primitive *Untermenschen* (sub-humans), meaning Slavs and other so-called inferior races, supposedly ruled by Jewish Bolsheviks. It was an asserted Nazi policy to exterminate Russians and all people of Slavic origin or, alternatively, to deport them and use them as slave labor. Slavs were to become the future underlings of the new Aryan rulers. Manufacturing was to take place in the central German industrial areas, while the other European countries were to serve as suppliers of raw materials on the one hand and as the market for German products on the other. Norway's most important economic contribution to this plan was intended to be fish and energy.

But obtaining fresh fish urgently required the development and optimization of production methods, as well as proximity to fresh supplies. Northern Norway was the center of the huge annual catches of cod and herring. As far as fish products for the fighting German army and the wider German population were concerned, the problem of transportation was paramount. In this sense, the German occupation served as a catalyst to solve the problems of Norway's fishing industry, which had developed in the interwar years and the Great Depression. The construction of roads and railroads became vital to fish exports and the expansion and development of the frozen fish industry. Throughout these years, the phrase *Fresch Fisch aus Norwegen* (fresh fish from Norway) could be seen stenciled on the railroad cars that came from Trondheim through Oslo on their way to Germany.

The town of Trondheim occupied an important place in Nazi Germany's long-term plans. On August 13, 1940, in a letter to Josef Terboven, *Reichskommissar* for Norway, Albert Speer wrote that the führer wished to let a German architect build a whole new Trondheim and "that here, as he expressed it, he imagines the creation of the great Reich's northernmost cultural center." Hitler personally sketched plans for the main roads and a railroad that would connect first Berlin and Trondheim and, later, cross the Arctic Circle on to Narvik and the North Cape. In their 2012 book *Himmlers Norge* (Himmler's Norway), Terje Emberland and Matthew Kott show how Adolf Hitler was personally preoccupied by Norway as something more than a militarily useful and strategically placed country. He regarded Norway and Norwegians as an integral part of the new Pan-Germanic Reich, with Trondheim at its center.

The export and import business in Norway had been paralyzed during the invasion and the following two months of fighting between

Norwegians and Nazi Germany. After the Norwegian capitulation on June 10, it was made clear that an occupied Norway would have its import needs supplied only by Germany or German-occupied areas. Goods imported for use in Norway from German-held areas were to be paid for with exported goods, mainly in tons of Norwegian fish.

Even before the invasion planned for April 9, Nazi Germany had laid the groundwork for control of the rich Norwegian resources. Norway and Germany had extensive commercial relations in the fish and fish products trade before 1940, with more than 40 percent of Norway's fish exports going to Germany in 1938. Transportation was briefly interrupted after the invasion, but negotiations between the Germans and Norwegians concerning cooperation in the fishing industry began whilst military battles were still being waged throughout the spring and summer of 1940. Following Norway's formal capitulation, plans for cooperation within the fisheries and other industries were settled. The main goal was to keep the wheels of commerce turning. With that in mind, the German authorities worked with the private sector to re-establish fish exports to Germany, to increase the catch, and to divert the exports that had previously gone to "enemy countries," primarily England. The German troops stationed in Norway also had to be provided with fish. Initially, German firms purchased all available stores of Norwegian canned goods to be delivered to the front. As early as August 1940 an agreement was reached between Norges Råfisklag (the Norwegian Fresh Fish Association) and German fish importers for the delivery of 150,000 tons of fresh fish; this agreement was expanded in December to 200,000 tons.

The arrangements changed with the arrival of Josef Terboven as head of the Norway *Reichskommissariat* in September. The Reichskommissariat set up its own Department of Fisheries under Herbst Vogt, with a subsection responsible for fisheries management (*Abteilung Fischwirtschaft.*) Plans included injecting German capital into the production of fish products and the complete reconstruction of the fisheries. This primarily involved integration into the German market and a shift in priorities from dried and salted fish to fresh and frozen fish exports. The Germans had little interest in dried or salted fish (*klippfisk*), and the goal was therefore to increase exports of fresh fish, which were in higher demand in the German market. Preparations were made for German investment in the fishing industry, including freezing and canning facilities, to ensure both volume and quality.

Frostfilet Established in Trondheim

On March 7, 1940, a few weeks before the German occupation, the corporation Frostfilet A/S was formally established in Trondheim to develop frozen fish fillet production. Even before its formal establishment, a customs exemption had already been requested for importing deep freezing equipment from Germany, specifically compressors for the creation of cold temperatures and filleting and skin removal machinery.

The first of the four German-owned freezer facilities established in Norway during the war, Frostfilet had its roots in the 1930s in Trondheim, where Necolai Dahl, in cooperation with David Ekker, began developing deep-freeze technology. German influence and direction were evident from the outset. Nordsee Deutsche Hochseefischerei (North Sea German High Seas Fisheries), one of the world's largest fishery enterprises with bases in Bremerhaven and Cuxhaven, was involved in the planning phase and became the principal stockholder in the Trondheim company. Köser, Platzman & Co. was another major stockholder. Ekker's and Dahl's own enterprises were also among the company's owners.

Shortly after the invasion, the Trondheim factory was inaugurated with a Norwegian workforce. The facility had a daily production capacity of seventy tons of finished fillet products. Filleting was carried out partly by machine and partly by hand. By 1943, 256 Norwegian men and 74 women were recorded as working in production, while 21 Norwegian men and women were employed in the offices. Additionally, twenty Germans were working at the facility at that time. The company had its own shipping department and, by 1945, owned nine ships, all named after fish, such as *Makrel* (mackerel) and *Kveita* (halibut).

From the beginning, the German government exerted its influence over the enterprise, making it clear that the factory's primary objective was to supply the German military's field kitchens. Between April 6 and August 14, 1940, twenty-nine customs declarations were made regarding import/export activities between Frostfilet A/S and Germany. Shipments of cellophane and cardboard, key materials for packaging frozen fish, arrived by ship and rail from Berlin, Dresden, and Oppeln. Customs records show that the first shipments reached Trondheim on April 9, 1940—the very day of the German invasion of Norway. By June 1940, frozen fish production was already well underway. Just five days before Norway's surrender on June 10, approximately 780 cartons of frozen cod fillets were shipped by rail from Trondheim to Germany. One week after the surrender, a further 595 cartons of frozen pollock fillets were dispatched. In total, eight shipments of frozen cod and pollock were sent to Germany between June 8 and 28, 1940.

8

TO REMAKE AN INDUSTRY

Germany had comprehensive plans for developing improved fish products in northern Norway. Implicit in the German fisheries policy was a focus on long-term development. German leaders were great admirers of Norwegian primary commodities but regarded these enterprises as underdeveloped. Fishermen and farmers were considered select groups destined for a better standard of living after the occupation. Production needed to be modernized and profits increased. The German leadership believed there was a genuine need to improve frozen fish products, thereby commanding higher prices. The Reichskommissariat's first annual report reveals the Germans' view of their own role in this process—namely, that such a massive transformation of the Norwegian fishing industry could only occur under German tutelage and capital investment.

Beyond the strategic considerations, there were clear ideological motives underlying Nazi Germany's approach. The German occupation of Norway would, by increasing the production of processed fish, create employment opportunities and thereby encourage population growth in northern Norway. This was seen as essential to protecting the genetic integrity of the "Nordic-Germanic" people in the area. Elements within the German administration regarded Norwegian farmers and fishermen as Aryans who constituted an untainted bastion against the international world of non-Aryan finance: according to Nazi racial ideology, Norway and Sweden had not been subject to the same degree of racial mixing as other parts of Scandinavia. While this ideology may have mattered less beyond the desks of the German leadership, it nonetheless aligned with the importance they placed on primary commodities.

Within the Norwegian fishing community, however, this ideology met with significant resistance. Traditionally, fishermen were admired as independent small producers, and the idea that German capital and technology might "liberate" them clashed with their long-standing rejection of corporate involvement in their work. The views of Norwegian fishermen contrasted sharply with those of the German fishing industry, which relied on modern, large-scale freezer facilities and trawler fleets backed by substantial financial investment. Financially strong companies played a central role in northern Norway, bringing capital and German industrial innovations. These firms invested fully or in part, buying corporate shares in Norwegian companies and introducing modern technology.

A fishing boat belonging to Frostfilet A/S, Trondheim. (Photo: Unknown.)

Divergent viewpoints within the German camp and contradictions among various Norwegian stakeholders would influence future developments. Everyone depended on everyone else. For Germany to obtain fish from Norway, fuel was required to supply the fishing vessels, and energy was needed to run the factories. The fish had to be purchased and transported to processing facilities, and subsequently shipped onward, primarily to Germany. The *Fischeinkaufgemeinschaft* (fish purchasing companies) were established by the German government in Berlin in the fall of 1940, under the auspices of the *Reichswirtschaftsministerium* (Reich Ministry of Economy). This organization controlled both German import companies and the German fish processing facilities in Norway. Purchases by the frozen fish factories were governed by the rules of *Fischeinkauf,* as it was commonly referred to.

The Norwegian fishing fleet, composed of small- and medium-sized vessels, was the primary supplier of fish to the German filleting factories. All types of boats were used, and the cod-fishing season provided employment for many. During this season, Norwegian collector vessels received fish from smaller fishing boats at Røst, and the Lofoten and Vesterålen Islands, transporting the catch to filleting factories. In some locations, fishermen delivered fish directly to the Germans. Fishermen had no control over whether the catch was used to feed the Norwegian population, supply the Wehrmacht in Norway, or sold to Fischeinkaufgemeinschaft Norwegen. The Germans were known to pay more than Norwegian buyers, and a local maxim proposed, "Freighter captains are like camel owners in a time of war," profiting considerably during the five years of German occupation.

Fish Factories in Nordland

Trondheim is in the southern third of Norway. Farther north, three facilities were in operation at the outset of the war, at Bodø, Melbu, and Hammerfest. The Germans quickly became interested in these facilities.

Bodø

In Bodø, the largest town and administrative center of Nordland County, the Germans began negotiations with the Schjølberg brothers, Eilert and Ragnar, who operated a fisheries enterprise at nearby Langstranda. The factory, established in 1930, featured four refrigeration units for salted and dried fish, as well as a brine freezer using ice and salt for freezing bait herring.

The Allies' appreciation of the importance of the fishing industry to the German war effort is evident from the fact that the facility in Bodø was bombed by the Allies in May 1940, though it was quickly rebuilt.

Several undated historical documents authored by Ragnar and Eilert Schjølberg describe the negotiations between the Germans and the Schjølberg enterprise. In a letter to the *Direktoratet for fiendtlig formue* (Directorate of Enemy Fortune) dated August 2, 1945, and signed by barrister Olav Angell, the brothers explain how they were forced into a contract with Nordsee.

On October 22, 1940, two German engineers, C. Keysler and O. Böttger, arrived and established their offices at Langstranda. An extensive agreement was signed between Ragnar Schjølberg and the occupation authorities on December 2, 1940. The German companies already behind Frostfilet A/S were the official signatories, but the involvement of Major Vilhelm Roloff of the Wehrmacht High Command revealed the direct engagement of significant German military interests. The agreement granted the Germans control over the most critical parts of the facilities and the right to construct additional production units if necessary—which they did in the spring of 1941.

The construction work proceeded rapidly despite the lack of qualified labor, principally using Norwegian labor, although an imported Spanish workforce was also employed. This became the Bodø Frostfilet A/S factory, beginning operations in summer of 1941.

The factory was considered to be the most modern fishery facility in Europe, equipped with filleting machines, freezer units, and a highly advanced laboratory. One report described the factory as follows: "The Bodø installation has fourteen Birds-Eye [flash-freezing] units and is probably, with its capacity of 120–130 tons per day in three shifts, Europe's, if not the world's, biggest."

Aerial view of Bodø, showing the Frostfilet complex on the left and the hospital and labor camp in the middle ground, with Bodø and the mountains in the background. (Photo: Unknown.)

This new facility processed all components of the catch, ensuring that nothing went to waste. Fish by-products were delivered to the country's fur farmers for use as feed. The facility produced frozen fish fillets, fishmeal, fish paste, and canned fish. It also housed a cod-liver oil steam extractor and included a factory for assembling fish boxes and manufacturing metal cans for canned fish.

Notably, the factory employed so-called "tray freezers" under a patent owned by the Anglo-Dutch company Unilever, which received royalties for every kilo of frozen fish produced. In 1941, Unilever became a partner with Nordsee, thereby profiting further from the Frostfilet facilities in Norway. Paradoxically, it benefited from investments in a food supply chain that supported German soldiers fighting against British and Dutch interests.

In parallel with the development of the Bodø Frostfilet factories, a camp was constructed for the labor force. Additional infrastructure included housing for managers, a clinic, and barracks for Wehrmacht guards and security forces provided by the Hirden, the members of the paramilitary wing of the Norwegian fascist Nasjonal Samling party.

Housing for the German staff.

Newly built barracks for the workers, each planned for up to one hundred men.

Melbu

In Melbu, a village on the island of Hadseløya, a company owned by Gunnar Fredriksen operated a filleting factory equipped with a freezer unit. German interests acquired 99 percent of the company's shares, in agreement with Fredriksen, and a modern filleting facility was constructed with a freezing capacity of forty tons per day. German experts worked in the freezing department at this site. Two German engineers were employed: Ferdinand Flor headed operations, while Ulrich Beirich oversaw the machinery. A German statistician was also employed in the office. Production work, however, was carried out exclusively by Norwegian men and women.

Hammerfest

In Hammerfest, the biggest town in Finnmark County, the Germans constructed a new frozen fish factory called the Vereinigte Tiefkühlgesellschaften Lohmann & Co. (Vertilo). The owner, Heinz Lohmann, was an innovator in frozen fish production, with facilities in the German cities of Cuxhaven, Wesermünde, and Hamburg. The company had developed a freezing system in which fish were packed in waterproof aluminum casings and drizzled with powdered calcium brine.

Seeing an opportunity to exploit raw materials from the Barents Sea, in 1940 the company sent its representative Hans Roesler to Hammerfest. There, he presented to the town's authorities plans to construct a fish-filleting factory with an adjacent freezer unit. The company was granted permission by the county to rent the necessary site at Fuglenes, not far from the Meridian Monument, one of Hammerfest's most notable landmarks. This monument, a copper globe atop a marble column, was erected to commemorate the Russian astronomer and geodesist Friedrich Georg Wilhelm Struve's work in 1854. From 1816 to 1855, over a span of thirty-nine years, Struve conducted degree measurements across ten countries, from Ismael by the Black Sea to Fuglenes in Hammerfest—an endeavor crucial to understanding the earth's shape and size.

Construction of the factory began in January 1941, with production starting in June of the same year. The facility employed modern freezer technology and had a daily freezing capacity of fifty tons at minus eighteen degrees Celsius. Raw material was transported by rail from the dock to the filleting machines, while waste products were dried and used for fishmeal. The processed fish was packed into thirty-kilogram blocks and shipped to Germany via specialized vessels.

The Problem of Norwegian Labor

Despite these developments, Norway provided little expertise in industrial frozen fillet production. The frozen food industry was a relatively new innovation, and Norway lacked both experience and technical education in this type of production. In the 1920s and 1930s, frozen product manufacturing—particularly fish fillets—represented a golden opportunity in Norway. A national plan for freezing facilities was developed in 1932, but construction stalled due to a lack of capital investment. The breakthrough in industrial frozen fish production came with the German occupation and the substantial German investment in the north.

More broadly, vocational education in crafts and industry, including schools and apprenticeship programs, was underdeveloped in Norway in the 1930s. In 1935, the country had only ten preparatory schools for crafts and industry. By 1939, this number had grown to twenty-eight vocational schools. The war brought rapid expansion, and by 1945 there were forty-two such schools, all offering educational opportunities in crafts and industry. New facilities had to be built to accommodate these schools, requiring construction workers of all kinds.

Unemployment in Norway disappeared with the onset of the German occupation. Norway was the only occupied country that did not supply workers to the German Reich. In 1940, there was a great need for labor power in Norway—unlike in Denmark, where unemployment remained high. As a result, Danish workers were sent both to Germany and to Norway. However, it soon became clear that the Germans struggled to recruit dependable Norwegian labor for their frozen fish factories. The new plant at Langstranda required a large workforce of both men and women.

In a circular dated July 9, 1941, the Directorate of Employment issued a forced enrollment decree, mandating Norwegians to perform "work to help in tasks particularly important to social welfare."

Employment in the fishing industry was deemed to fall into this category, including work at Frostfilet in Trondheim and Bodø, Lohmann in Hammerfest, and the filleting plant at Melbu. Filleting, which was central to frozen fish production, was specifically highlighted, and women's smaller hands were considered particularly suited for the task.

In 1941, Norwegians were ordered to register for work, and about 30,000 did so over the course of the war. Men and women were recruited for the frozen fish plants in Bodø and Hammerfest, with part of the workforce coming from southern Norway. These southern workers were not well received in Bodø, being disparaged by the local population. Rumors circulated that young girls working at Frostfilet had social and sexual relationships with German soldiers, and that the "foreign workers" from the south brought contagious diseases. Medical reports from 1941 noted an increase in cases of impetigo, "worst among the newly arrived workers at the plant at Langstranda."

German records from the period reported significant challenges in recruiting Norwegians, and often referenced the poor work habits of those recruited. Both Norwegian and German authorities received frequent complaints about the Norwegian laborers. Some men were caught falsifying overtime claims and signatures or arriving late to work. Others simply failed to return after vacations, or did not show up at all.

The Germans claimed that the Norwegian laborers brought from the south lacked a work ethic and caused trouble from the outset. A letter sent in 1942 to the Reichskommissariat in Oslo complained about these so-called "devilish elements," suggesting that southern authorities were sending undesirable individuals to the north. German management in Hammerfest expressed hopes of returning these workers to the south. Efforts to conscript Norwegian labor—especially women—for filleting work were largely unsuccessful in Hammerfest, just as they had been at Langstranda and Melbu.

In January 1941, the Nordsee company placed advertisements in the *Cuxhaven Tagesblatt*, the newspaper of the German seaport town of Cuxhaven, seeking skilled labor for the fishing industry. The industry was clearly desperate.

9

THE FEMALE LABOR CONUNDRUM: IDEOLOGY VS. PRAGMATISM

Cleaning cod fillets in the Frostfilet factory at Langstranda. (Photo: Rolf Sander/The Nordland Museum.)

On February 16, 1942, Kittner raised the issue of the need for female labor. At that time, the Bodø Fish Plant employed only a hundred women, and needed more. It was proposed that maids working in Bodø for families without children, or with only one or two children, might be conscripted to work at Frostfilet. Detailed plans were drawn up. The women would pay rent for their accommodations, with the cost deducted from their salaries. At least another hundred female workers were needed. The situation was dire: fish was rotting due to the labor shortage. A telegram dated February 27 reveals that Eiler Prytz, the Quisling government's Minister of Nutrition, became involved. He informed the county commissioner in Bodø that Director Vilhelm Roloff would travel to Bodø and Frostfilet to resolve the issues. Once again, the Germans expressed concern about the "amoral behavior" of the Norwegian female workforce. Sexually transmitted diseases were a common concern for military commands during wartime. A health report dated November 28, 1942, stated:

> Some of the female workers, most between seventeen and twenty-five years old, conduct a most immoral activity during their night shifts. The company directors therefore consistently complain that they do not show up for work. On the other hand, the Norwegian hospital complains about the large number of girls from this company with venereal disease. In addition, the Norwegian police complain about the number of investigations they must conduct because Norwegian seamen and German soldiers have been infected. When, for example, an investigation was launched after eleven young girls failed to report for work, it was discovered that they had spent several days aboard the ship *D.S. Mellum,* servicing Norwegians and Germans. The police brought the eleven girls to the hospital, and five of them were found to be infected with venereal disease. In this context, it must be noted that at Bodø Hospital there is a room known as "The Frostfilet Room," often occupied by girls with venereal disease.

In a letter to the German security service and Norwegian authorities in Bodø, dated July 9, 1942, the directors of Frostfilet reported that many women simply disappeared. Two women from Oslo and one from Tønsberg were found in Kristiansund and were returned to Bodø, where they were placed in quarantine. As efforts to reintegrate them into the workforce failed, it was suggested they be sent to an educational camp to be taught how to work.

Concluding that Norwegian female workers were difficult to discipline and unwilling to endure the demanding labor of the fish industry, the Germans began seeking alternative labor sources. This intention was confirmed in a report from the German secret police to Berlin, dated November 28, 1942. New sources of female labor were to be found in the occupied territories of the East.

A Woman's Place?

The solution to this problem demonstrated the hypocrisy and cruelty of Nazi policy. Whereas the Soviet Union vacillated on how to answer the so-called "woman question" (did women belong in the home and/or the labor market?), National Socialism adopted a much less ambiguous stance: women had no place in the male sphere of war and battle, as defined by Nazi ideology. A woman's role was to give birth to Aryan children. Through childbirth, she contributed to the fatherland by producing future soldiers. This ideology culminated during World War II in the awarding of the infamous Mother's Cross, wrought in gold, silver, or bronze, to German women based on the number of children—and therefore future soldiers—they gave birth to.

The "woman question" has been one of the most controversial debates throughout the development of industrialization, whether in Germany, Norway, or elsewhere. Views on women's roles in the home versus the labor market have often fluctuated in response to economic cycles, with public rhetoric shifting accordingly. These questions remained prominent in the postwar years and were not far removed from the ideas Adolf Hitler espoused in the 1920s—though, of course, without the same brutal consequences seen in Nazi Germany.

In the Third Reich, the concepts of women's equality and the right to work were effectively erased. Hitler's view of a woman's rightful place was encapsulated in the slogan *Kinder, Kirche, Küche* (children, church, kitchen). In chapter 1 of *Mein Kampf,* he wrote: "Little girl, remember that you are to become a German mother." Hitler denounced the idea of women being socially and sexually liberated, an idea associated with socialist and Marxist movements since the rise of industrial capitalism and the working class. In his view, the driving force of world history was not class struggle but racial struggle. Women had a defined role in this battle: biology was destiny.

Thus, biological determinism replaced earlier historical frameworks centered on class or production. This ideology was articulated clearly in Hitler's speech to the National Socialist Women's League (NS-Frauenschaft) on September 15, 1935:

The so-called granting of equal rights to women which Marxism demands, in reality does not give equal rights but constitutes a deprivation of rights, since it draws the woman into an area in which she will necessarily be inferior.... I would be ashamed to be a German man even if only one woman had to go to the front. The woman has her own battlefield. With every child she brings into the world, she fights her battle for the nation. The man stands up for the *Volk*...as the woman stands up for her family.

In general, these views on women were rooted in and reinforced by the bourgeois morality of the early twentieth century, which idealized the sanctity of the family. Women were expected to lead modest, devoted domestic lives. Which raises a fundamental question: how did the Nazis manage to secure the consent of millions of women for a political agenda so defined by a rigid gender division of labor and blatant patriarchy? In her 1987 book, *Mothers in the Fatherland: Women, the Family, and Nazi Politics,* historian Claudia Koonz argued that across class divisions, vast numbers of German women became complicit in—and supportive of—laws that emphasized race and institutionalized gender polarity. German women in Hitler's Reich found themselves trapped in a web of conformity and repression they had helped to create.

However, the Third Reich was willing to compromise its ideals regarding women's place in the domestic sphere when the women in question were considered racially inferior, as was the case with Slavic peoples. Ruled by the despised Jewish Bolsheviks, these women were viewed as *Untermenschen* (sub-humans), and Nazi policy called for their extermination or deportation for use as forced laborers. In total, more than a million Soviet women were abducted and forced to work in Germany and in occupied territories, including Norway.

By contrast, Norwegian women, though often regarded as undisciplined workers, were seen as essential to Nazi plans for a racial empire. This perspective was shaped by Nazi racial ideology and eugenics theory, which held that Nordic women could contribute to the biological and demographic goals of the regime.

The *Lebensborn* Program

In the same way that many women in Germany supported the Nazi Party, in Norway women supported its equivalent, the Nasjonal Samling (National Union). In fact, a significant proportion of party members in Norway were women. Norwegian women also played a crucial role in Nazi Germany's plan for a racial empire. After the Soviet Union was to be "cleansed" of so-called inferior races, the conquered lands were intended to be repopulated with "Nordic Aryans." Within this vision, it was considered desirable for Norwegian women and aristocratic German men to produce the Aryan children of the future. A central element of this plan was the *Lebensborn* ("Fount of Life") program, initiated in Germany in 1935 by Heinrich Himmler. The program aimed to increase the number of Aryan births and combat Germany's declining birthrate, thereby strengthening the racial health of the German population.

Himmler opened the first Lebensborn home in Steinhöring, near Munich, in August 1936. The program focused on the care of pregnant women deemed to have desirable racial and biological traits, and expected to give birth to the ideal Aryan: "perfect stallions, at least one meter and eighty centimeters tall, blond and blue-eyed, muscles bulging, and sleek, disciplined Spartans." Initially, the Lebensborn program targeted single Aryan mothers, promising them secrecy, protection, and adoptive homes for their newborns among approved SS families. It represented the ideological mirror of the SS's genocidal policies, both aiming to refine Europe's racial makeup, through either selective breeding or the elimination of perceived genetic threats.

Lebensborn homes were eventually established across Germany and Austria, as well as in occupied countries, including Norway. In December 1940, SS leader and Gestapo chief in Norway Wilhelm Rediess, working closely with Reichskommissar Josef Terboven, wrote to Himmler regarding the anticipated wave of births from German soldiers stationed in Norway. Rediess sought to secure these children as assets of the Reich and, with Terboven's strong support, proposed establishing Lebensborn facilities in Norway. Norwegian women, in the eyes of the Nazi Party, were not producing enough children.

In February 1941, Himmler, Terboven, and Wehrmacht commanders in Norway convened and agreed to establish a branch of the Lebensborn program to care for the children of German soldiers. With the need for accommodations becoming urgent by the spring of 1941, Lebensborn authorities began acquiring and repurposing buildings for their mission. In August 1941, the first facility opened at Hurdal Verk, a former resort with a private park and manor house located north of Oslo. This was the first Lebensborn home established outside of Germany and Austria. During the war, twelve Lebensborn facilities were opened in Norway, more than in Germany itself. Locations included Geilo, Klekken, Hop near Bergen, Godthaap near Oslo, and Trondheim, among others. These homes housed Norwegian women, and their staff consisted of both German and Norwegian personnel.

Twelve thousand children were born in Lebensborn homes in Norway. Many of them were later sent to special homes in Germany to make sure they received a "proper" Aryan upbringing. These children were intended to become future leaders, charged with advancing the Aryan race. They were to be granted agricultural land in the East, within the Greater Germanic Reich, once it had been fully conquered. Norwegians, both men and women, were expected to participate actively in the development of these territories seized from the Soviet Union. This line of reasoning influenced Nazi strategies across Europe, particularly in the Soviet Union.

For most of the children born under such unfortunate circumstances, Lebensborn ended in a nightmare. In her novel *Trieste* (2007), writer Daša Drndić wrote powerfully about these difficult legacies: "Norway, where this was a flourishing activity and from whence today there is a little army, not of baby boomers, but of baby doomers, about 12,000 all told, born between 1942 and 1945."

The first Lebensborn mother and birthcare home in Norway, Hurdal Verk, in September 1941 just a few weeks after its opening. (Photo: Archives of Norway, in Wikimedia Commons/National.)

Tragically, these children, already tested by the Nazis to assess their genetic value, were again evaluated along similar lines by Norwegian authorities. As early as 1943, Norwegian politicians in exile in London formed a committee to determine the fate of the so-called "war children" after liberation. Physicians were hired to assess their mental fitness. A 1945 report from this War Children's Committee cited senior psychiatrist Ørnulf Ødegaard, who, based on his observations of around thirty-five "German girls" treated at Gaustad Hospital during the war, estimated that 2,500 of the approximately 9,000 children would suffer from "mental defects," particularly mental retardation. This grim prediction implied that the children would become a long-term burden on the Norwegian welfare system. Their mothers were often subjected to harsh stigma, frequently referred to as "sluts" who had betrayed Norway with their bodies.

In more recent years, the "skewed and pseudoscientific descriptions of the war children and their mothers from the years immediately following the war" have been re-evaluated through rigorous social research. Available data indicate that these vulnerable and stigmatized children were more likely to become part of socially marginalized groups, as evidenced by higher mortality rates and early receipt of disability pensions. As researcher Dag Ellingsen bluntly put it: "there was a clear expectation that the 'German kids' would not fare well, and for many, this is what happened."

Over the years, these children were often bullied and mistreated; many lived as outcasts or were placed in orphanages and mental institutions. Eventually, efforts were made to seek redress for the injustices inflicted on them and their mothers. In 2001, an association of Lebensborn children sued the Norwegian Government for violation of their human rights and initially won in court. However, the case was later dismissed on the grounds that too much time had passed for the claim to remain valid. The case then passed to the European Court of Human Rights in Strasbourg in 2007, with a similar result. It was only in 2018, at an event to commemorate the seventieth anniversary of the Universal Declaration of Human Rights, that Prime Minister Erna Solberg issued an apology and admitted that in the case of the Lebensborn women and children, "Norwegian authorities violated the fundamental principle that no citizen can be punished without trial or sentenced without law."

An Industry Dependent on Women

The decision to find female labor in the occupied territories of Eastern Europe and the Soviet Union, though demonstrably contrary to Nazi ideology about gender roles, was perfectly in keeping with economic and social history. Women have been part of the industrial workforce since the beginning of industrialization. They have worked on production lines and operated machinery in factories since the inception of the assembly line. Women, along with children, were often placed in jobs requiring precision, dexterity, and repetitive actions performed at a fast pace. While industrial development progressed, a sharp and persistent divide remained between what was considered "women's work" and "men's work."

Although women have operated machinery, a distinct hierarchy was maintained in crafts and industry professions among what was considered skilled, semi-skilled, and unskilled labor. Men, women, and children were frequently pitted against each other in conflicts over job access and wages. Despite receiving lower pay, women and children were considered desirable labor sources for specific roles. The struggle for women's right to professional education in crafts and industry has seen significant progress only in recent decades.

In Norway's fishing industry, filleting work reflected the common gender divisions found in other forms of assembly-line production. For both male and female factory workers, gender-based labor roles were often accepted as part of the natural order—just the way it had always been. In food industries more broadly, assembly-line labor has traditionally been performed by women.

In northern Norway, as in other fishing communities, women traditionally worked seasonally. Their roles typically involved cutting, weighing, and packing fish. Gender segregation in the workplace often meant that men and women worked in areas of production that were physically separated. However, men were frequently placed in supervisory roles over women's production lines, reinforcing long-standing assumptions about gendered labor.

Men were assigned more varied tasks that required higher qualifications. In the fishing industry, men traditionally occupied key roles on boats, in management, and on the docks. They were also responsible for servicing machinery, tasks requiring knowledge in fields such as electricity and mechanics, which were long reserved for men. Food production industries, including the frozen fish sector, have generally paid low wages, and the Norwegian fishing industry followed this pattern.

However, this new industry faced specific logistical challenges. Labor had to be available immediately upon the arrival of fresh fish, as delays meant spoilage: fish rots quickly. Norwegian women had proven to be an unreliable labor source in this context. Consequently, the Germans began seeking new solutions to meet their production demands.

Reversing the Hunger Plan

All of the above must be consider within the wider context of the Third Reich's overall prosecution of the war. After a period of murder and brutality against both prisoners of war and the civilian population, the Germans gradually changed their perspective on the people of the conquered countries in Eastern Europe, beginning to view them as an enormous reservoir of slave labor. The deficit of millions of workers in German industry and agriculture came to outweigh Nazi objections to the use of Slavs as a source of labor. An order from the leadership, signed by Field Marshal Wilhelm Keitel on October 31, 1941, paved the way for the full exploitation of Soviet prisoners of war in the German war economy.

Until that time, the Germans had been using their "Hunger Plan" as part of their war strategy. One part of the Nazi plan for the future of Ukraine and South Russia concerned their rich agricultural areas, which would provide the German people with *Lebensraum* and food. The Slavic population was to cease to exist. Death by starvation was one method of elimination, and another was literally working Slavic captives to death. Approximately 1.3 million prisoners of war died in this way during the first four months of the invasion.

However, the lack of available labor in Germany and the occupied territories necessitated a change in strategy. In 1941–42, the idea of recruiting prisoners of war and youth from the Soviet Union for labor purposes began to take hold. It was important to keep weapons production going as workers in the German armaments industry were drafted and sent to the front. Germany also lacked agricultural laborers. In March 1942, a special office of work allocation, Generalbevollmächtigter für den Arbeitseinsatz (GBA), was established, with one of Hitler's old party comrades, Fritz Sauckel, at the helm. He announced that his goal was to supply millions of foreign workers for Germany's war economy and make them work to their utmost capacity. The need for labor was insatiable.

In the spring of 1942, the mass deportation of youths from Ukraine, Belarus, and the occupied parts of Russia began. With the cooperation of local police, the Wehrmacht entered towns and villages and carried away boys and girls. They were brought to the nearest railroad station and loaded into cattle cars, bound for destinations unknown. Eight to ten thousand youths were shipped out every week during the spring of 1942. This marked the beginning of countless young people from Russia, Belarus, and Ukraine being sent to Germany—and, in some cases, to Norway, and into frozen fish production.

The scale of enslavement is almost unimaginable today. By August 1944, there were 7,615,970 registered forced laborers in Greater Germany, of whom 1.9 million were prisoners of war. Approximately 5.7 million were civilian forced laborers, and of these, 2.8 million were from the Soviet Union. Almost half of them were women.

More than 120,000 were sent to Norway, including over 100,000 soldiers of the Red Army. The rest were so-called *Ostarbeiter*—eastern workers. Galina Korolenko and Fedor Salnikov were among them, along with several other young people we are about to meet.

PART III

THE FACTORIES

10

THE "EASTERN WORKERS" ARRIVE

In early June 1942, a ship docked in Bodø, disembarking civilians from Russia, Belarus, and Ukraine who had been conscripted by German troops. Among the arrivals were also Soviet prisoners of war.

Many individuals from both groups were sent to Langstranda, not far from Bodø. In a telegram sent on September 12, 1942, to the Department of the Interior in Oslo, the County Commissioner of Nordland stated that the company had 750 Soviet and 250 Norwegian workers and that, when fully operational, it would employ 1,500 workers.

It should be borne in mind that figures and data regarding the workforce at Frostfilet are unreliable and sometimes contradictory. They vary from one document to the next, and it is difficult to find consistent information about the arrival of the different groups. As noted previously, the German occupiers and their Norwegian Nazi allies used the term *Ostarbeiter* ("eastern workers"), a euphemism applied in the Eastern Workers' Decrees announced by Heinrich Himmler on February 20, 1942. These decrees eventually encompassed over three million Soviet workers put to work across the Third Reich and the territories it occupied. The Norwegian authorities, by contrast, used the more accurate term *sivile tvangsarbeidere* (forced civilian laborers).

It seems clear that most of the laborers were from Ukraine and Russia, with a few from Belarus. However, lists of those registered at Langstranda in 1945 prior to repatriation also included Poles, Czechs, Bulgarians, and Lithuanians. From the Balkans, there were men from Croatia, Serbia, and Macedonia. The oldest of the men was fifty when he arrived in Norway, while the youngest was born in 1926 and had been just fifteen when Germany invaded the Soviet Union.

Who, and From Where?

Group photo of men at Frostfilet A/S at Langstranda near Bodø, Spring of 1945. (Photo courtesy Yuri Salnikov.)

More broadly, across the 500 prison camps built by the Germans in Norway, the majority of the inmates came from the vast regions of the East. The Soviet Union was a kaleidoscope of different ethnic groups, and this was reflected in the prisoner population. When the prisoners finally returned to the Soviet Union in 1945, fifty-five ethnic groups were registered as Soviet citizens. The majority were Russians (65 percent), 27 percent were Ukrainians, and 5.5 percent were Byelorussians. These individuals came from different social backgrounds and held varying political viewpoints. They spoke different languages, and had different historical roots and experiences. Some supported the

October Revolution; some were supporters of Andrei Vlasov, the turncoat Red Army general; and some were members of the Soviet secret police, known by its Russian abbreviation, NKVD. One of the latter, Arkady Mihailovich Mozyerin, fathered a child with another prisoner, Marfa Maksimovna Stepina, whom we will meet in the following chapter.

Many were brought to Norway by Organisation Todt, the massive engineering enterprise responsible for constructing military installations across Germany and the occupied countries. It employed Soviet women in a variety of roles in Norway. Later, in 1945, the Soviet Union's Repatriation Commission documented the return of 1,309 Soviet women over the age of fourteen and 389 children under the age of sixteen who had labored for the German Reich in different parts of the country. Their "recruitment" had been organized, in part, through Organisation Todt. Some were just fourteen when they arrived. They were placed throughout the country and worked in food preparation and cleaning at various Wehrmacht installations. Approximately 1,000 women worked for the Luftwaffe, and forty worked in aluminum production at Nordag.

Organisation Todt took its name from its founder and leader, Fritz Todt, former Inspector General for German Roadways, whose most important task had been the development of the German motorways. The Organisation Todt district office in Oslo covered both Denmark and Norway and was administered by Einsatzgruppe Wiking. However, the office responsible for supplying labor for the fishing industry was directly administered by the Reichskommissariat's Department of Nutrition.

The Women at Langstranda

Ascertaining the exact number of women at Langstranda is difficult. However, production records dated June 30, 1943, state that in July of that year, the plant had 760 *Ostarbeiter*, ninety-nine of whom were women, and 120 Norwegians, in addition to approximately 100 Germans. This was the first mention of female forced laborers According to the document, the oldest were Anna Kuanja from

Mohilev, who was fifty-seven years old in 1945, and Marija Karpunina from Orel, aged forty-six. The two youngest were eighteen-year-old Marija Palova from Smolensk and seventeen-year-old Marija Laiseva from Orel in 1945 (names as written in the document).

The archives in Trondheim provided more information about the Frostfilet prisoners than those in Bodø, and show that many of the women arrived later than the men—in 1943 rather than 1942. In a letter dated January 10, 1943, Wehrmachtbefehlshaber (military commander) Steltzer stated that 250 "Ukrainian women" were expected to arrive in Oslo on January 19, 1943. Of these, one hundred were to be sent to Hochseefischerei A.G. Nordsee in Bodø, and 150 were destined for the Lohmann factory in Hammerfest. Lieutenant-Colonel Steltzer asked the Organisation Todt office in Trondheim to reserve places on the coastal steamer from Trondheim to Bodø and Hammerfest. He also requested information about the ship's departure time from Trondheim so the journey from Oslo could be coordinated. It is possible that Galina was on the train to Trondheim and then on the ship to Bodø.

In the letter, all the women are referred to as Ukrainians. However, closer inspection reveals that this was not entirely accurate. While most of the women who came to Hammerfest starting in June 1942 were from Ukraine, others were from Russia and Belarus. Some of the women prisoners were put to work outside the camp, performing cleaning and housekeeping duties in the living quarters of the Wehrmacht and the intelligence services (*Sicherheitsdienst* or SD).

There is some debate as to whether the Ukrainian female workers came voluntarily. This may have been the case for a few of them. In Ukraine, people had experienced oppression, persecution, deportation, and famine during the 1930s. Many did not feel sympathetic toward Soviet authorities. According to an eyewitness from Minsk, Belarus: "Some people wearing embroidered folk costumes greeted the Germans with bread and salt. With joy. Many people thought, 'Here come the Germans—now we can live a normal life.' Many were opposed to the USSR and General Josef Stalin."

Some took an active role in the persecution of Jews, which began immediately after the invasion. Others helped hide Jewish families. Although the complete eradication of the Jewish people was formally approved during the Wannsee Conference on January 20, 1942, mass killings had already begun earlier in the occupied areas of the East. Local populations and police cooperated with the SS in eliminating what they called "undesirable elements."

Local police also actively participated in the rounding up and deportation of youth, both in Russia and in Belarus and Ukraine. At the same time, a growing resistance movement was developing—one that went underground and fought the occupiers. All these contradictions and conflicts were present in the prison camps throughout Norway, as we shall later see.

11

WORK IN THE FROSTFILET FACTORY

The Frostfilet complex. The buildings on the left held refrigeration units and storage facilities, while those on the right were the fish filleting and the fish paste production facilities. (Source for this and the following photos in this chapter: Rolf Sander/The Nordland Museum.)

A great deal of what we know about life and work in Langstranda during these years comes from two sources: a photo album collected by a German employee named Rolf Sander, and a set of drawings by a mysterious figure known only by his first name, Dimitrij (these drawings are discussed in the following chapter).

The photo album was donated to the Nordland Museum in 2011 by a relative of Sander living near Cuxhaven, Germany, a city long associated with the fishing industry (see previous chapter). Many of the photos show the extensive construction undertaken at Langstranda in 1941, before the arrival of the forced laborers, while others focus on the equipment and activities in the factory. Of particular interest is the depiction of the full cycle of production—from the arrival of the fish at the dock to their finishing as frozen fillets ready for dispatch.

The plant had four departments, producing respectively fillets, fish paste, fish meal (a commercial product used to feed farm animals), and fish oil. The photo album shows it as a place of large working spaces, harsh electric lighting, heavy machinery, and meticulously organized production lines. Norwegians worked mostly in the canning sector and the laboratory. The male prisoners worked where the fish were unloaded and in the refrigeration area. The women worked in the fish cutting, filleting, and packing sectors. The management in both was German.

Freshly caught fish is unloaded from the fishing cutter Rusken.

A sequence of photos shows boxes of fresh cod being unloaded from the fishing vessel *Rusken*, carried by sling from its hold to the dock, where they were sorted and distributed to the various production sectors of the factory.

A white-coated German manager checks the quality of the fish visually and by the time-honored method of sniffing the catch up close.

A white-coated manager checks the quality of the incoming fish.

When we move into the factory itself, men are seen removing bones from the fish by hand with sharp knives.

Hand filleting by male workers, a cold and dirty activity.

The fillets move by conveyor belt to the cutting and filleting area, where women take over. Some tasks, such as removing the skin from the fillets, are done by machine, but most of the weighing, cleaning, and packing is done by hand before the fish are moved in aluminum trays to the packing line. (Fish too small for standard packing are diverted to a separate line for cleaning and packing in smaller boxes.)

Weighing the cleaned fillets.

There, cardboard cartons containing nine kilos of finished fillets are assembled and covered with cellophane. At that point, the male workers return to the process, moving the cartons on aluminum trays to a long room containing the factory's fourteen upright freezers and the compressors that run them. After freezing, cardboard boxes containing four cartons each are stacked and stored in a deep-freeze area.

The photo sequence ends with the boxes being loaded at the Langstranda dock onto the refrigerator ship *Oldenburg,* ready to be transported to Cuxhaven.

12

LIFE BEHIND BARBED WIRE

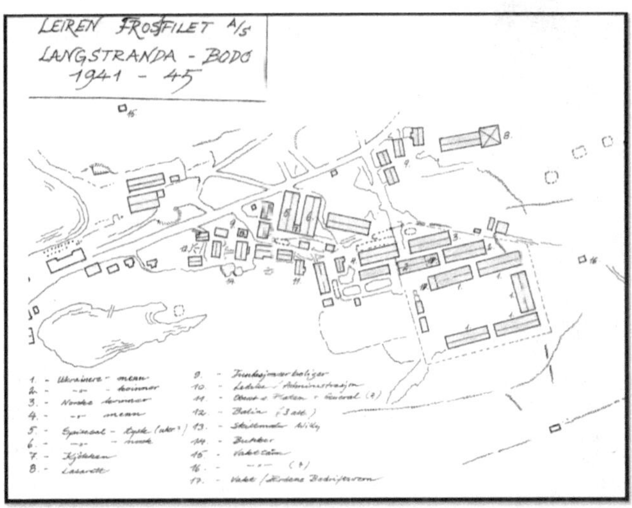

Map of the Langstranda prison camp hand-drawn by Knut Støre, with original legend.

Though the Sander photo album shows many faces, it is primarily a record of equipment and production processes rather than human stories. The basic facts of living arrangements are known from various records and from the limited descriptions provided by some of the individuals mentioned elsewhere in this book. The prisoners lived in a camp near the factory, where most of them spent three years battling icy winds and volatile weather as they made their way back and forth between the prison camp and the fish plant. A map of the camp, drawn by historian Knut Støre (see below), shows barracks for Norwegian women and men, as well as for "Ukrainian" women and men, who were housed in separate quarters. The prisoners' barracks were surrounded by barbed wire and guard towers, all located approximately one kilometer from the factory.

An aerial bridge connected the camp to the original factory of the Schjølbergs, which employed only Norwegian labor. It had an apartment complex for its employees, located opposite the factory. However, the area around both facilities was land-mined and enclosed by a double barbed-wire fence, patrolled by armed guards and dogs.

"he young Ukrainian artist Dmitrij. (Photo: Johan Lundli/The Nordland Museum.)

But it is the pictures drawn by the Ukrainian forced laborer known only as Dimitrij that give us insight into everyday life in the prison camp. Dimitrij was originally from Chudniv, a town about 200 kilometers west of Kyiv, and had been brought to Norway in 1942, where he worked on several projects as a forced laborer. The only surviving photo of Dimitrij shows a stocky, youthful-looking man.

Most of what is known about him comes from the family of the Norwegian Johan Lungli, whom he met while helping to construct the German field hospital at Klungset. It was to Johan that he entrusted his drawings, which are now in the collection of the Salten Museum in the town of Fauske, east of Bodø.

These drawings illustrate the abduction of prisoners from Ukraine and chronicle daily life at Langstranda. Most of what is known about him comes from the family of the Norwegian Johan Lungli, whom he met while helping to construct the German field hospital at Klungset. It was to Johan that he entrusted his drawings, which are now in the collection of the Salten Museum in the town of Fauske, east of Bodø.

He wrote the date December 15, 1942, on the first of the twenty drawings, while the last is dated 1943. Some of the drawings also contain ironic texts that were purposefully intended to be cryptic: they were written not only in Cyrillic, but also in reverse—possibly to make them harder for non-Soviet individuals to read.

Unlike the photos in the Sander album, Dimitrij's colored pencil drawings express both humor and pathos, as well as a certain dogged stoicism. A first sequence of drawings depicts the brutal rounding up of forced laborers on the flat landscape of Ukraine. Laconic inscriptions in reversed Cyrillic provide ironic commentary, such as "A journey to Germany for six months" as the workers approach the red boxcars, and "First acquaintance" as green-uniformed soldiers wielding batons herd them onto the wagons while a military band plays.

The prisoners, under armed guard, are transported by ship to Norway. The location then shifts to the prison barracks at Langstranda, with mountains visible in the near distance. The red-painted wooden barracks are surrounded by a wire fence, and a watchtower stands in the background. "This is our school," Dimitrij comments.

Punishment and brutality are rife in the drawings. Another, titled "Our New German Education," shows workers gathered around a table while one is beaten by German soldiers. In "A German Cold Shower," a half-dressed worker is doused with a bucket of cold water by a pistol-wielding soldier. No other workers are seen in the three-tiered bunkbeds, suggesting the punishment may be for oversleeping.

In another drawing, titled "Little Hawk Gets Used to the Fact That There Is Little to Eat," laborers queuing for soup are tormented by a German officer carrying two enormous ladles, who has kicked over one of the soup pots; other pots have been emptied onto the ground or over the workers' heads. The next drawing shows a guard beating a laborer with the text, "The German soldier in a green uniform stands with a baton in his right hand, ready for battle."

A few drawings depict the production facilities in the factory and suggest both resistance and repression. In one, workers manning a conveyor belt hide fish under their jackets and in their pockets. Another shows a German soldier searching the workers and discovering that they have smuggled fish back to the barracks.

Dimitrij depicted the presence of women in the camp in two drawings. One shows seven male eastern workers lined up along a fence outside a building, eyeing two female workers as they emerge. One of the men holds a placard bearing the word "Selection." Another drawing shows men and women talking through the barbed-wire fence that separates the male and female barracks.

According to Johan Lungli, Dimitrij eventually disappeared in 1943. No one knew his fate; Lungli believed the young man attempted to escape to Sweden with a friend, but perished in the mountains near the border.

Conflict and Control

As suggested by Dimitrij's drawings, the Frostfilet factory and the prison camp were riddled with conflicts and confrontations. The Schjølberg brothers—the owners of Bodø Fish Plant, and partners in the German enterprise—frequently complained about the Soviet forced laborers. They claimed: "The Russians stole from the warehouses, and they hid stolen German merchandise in the air vents and behind the insulation, which they broke open." In their letters to the German authorities, the brothers described widespread subversion and theft, alleging that even their own Schjølberg factory next door was targeted.

There were also tensions between Norwegians and Soviet prisoners of war. Some Norwegians acted like masters and treated the prisoners as slaves. Certain prisoners became despised capos and informers, while others worked for the German security services as interpreters and agents. In contrast, some laborers engaged in acts of sabotage.

Each group had its own internal divisions. Prisoners from Yugoslavia, for instance, were caught in the bitter legacy of their homeland's ongoing conflict between Croatian Ustaše and Serbian Chetnik supporters. Control was tightly enforced at the Hammerfest factory, but Frostfilet at Langstranda was guarded with particular intensity.

The plant, located at the tip of a peninsula, was surrounded by barbed wire and mined to prevent sabotage or escape. As depicted in Dimitrij's drawings, the forced laborers passed a guardhouse at the plant exit, where they were routinely inspected after work. Smuggling fish back to the barracks was forbidden, and the guards used dogs specifically trained to detect fish hidden on prisoners' persons.

The prison camp itself was also heavily guarded, with watchtowers and patrols. Both Germans and Norwegians supervised the factory and the camp. Initially, guards came from the German Public Order Police (Ordnungspolizei, or ORPO), but later, Norwegian members of the Nazi Party assumed responsibility. The Norwegian protection force, established in 1943, consisted of SS-affiliated members of the Hirden, tasked with guarding industrial and state institutions against sabotage. These Norwegian security officers had been trained in Trondheim, and some had served on the Eastern front with the Wehrmacht. By late 1943, fifteen Norwegian guards were stationed at Frostfilet.

A local Norwegian worker, Harald Hansen, recalled that while the treatment the Germans dished out was not good, it was at least humane. However, he noted that conditions worsened after the arrival of the Norwegian Hird guards, who were unpopular among both the eastern laborers and the Norwegian civilian workers.

The tensions, strategies of survival, and shifting allegiances within this diverse mix of forced laborers were extremely complex. As mentioned, some prisoners collaborated with the Hirden and became capos—deeply resented figures among their fellow inmates.

Capos enjoyed greater freedom of movement and privileges, but their perceived betrayal made them targets. Sources suggest that some defectors were "taken care of" by their fellow prisoners during the workday. For instance, a Croatian prisoner, Anton Staminki, suddenly disappeared; it was rumored that he had been beaten to death behind the camp. One capo was allegedly wrapped in barbed wire, dipped in tar, and "disappeared." Another was said to have been thrown into one of the hammermills used to grind fish. When he was reported missing, suspicion turned to certainty. The gruesome rumor became a national concern when a ship loaded with frozen fish was halted en route to Germany. It had been reported that the body of a prisoner might have been ground into the cargo. Samples were taken, and the rumor was confirmed. The entire cargo was returned to Bodø and destroyed.

The plant was also the target of bombing raids and acts of sabotage. The first act of sabotage occurred as early as May 1941, when parts of the plant burned down just before it was scheduled to open. Allied activities also took their toll and posed a danger to all. On September 12, 1941, a British Albacore plane launched an aerial torpedo toward the well-lit factory. Although the torpedo did not explode, it still managed to halt production for several days while experts were brought in from the south to neutralize it.

German military intelligence, the Abwehr, also conducted secret operations from the factory premises for a period of time. Security precautions were taken to prevent sabotage, and mines were placed around the site. In September 1943, a tragic accident occurred when a young couple from the prison camp stepped on a mine while walking near the beach. Anna Mischufkina from Russia died instantly. Theodor Nikolyn from Ukraine succumbed to his injuries the following day, on September 7, 1943.

Sabotage by Laborers

In all types of production, sabotage was a common problem during the Nazi occupation, whether carried out by prisoners of war or Norwegians. For example, documents describe acts of sabotage at the fish plant in Melbu, in Vesterålen north of Bodø, where only Norwegians were employed on the production line.

Gunnar Fredriksen's fishing company at Melbu generally had difficulty recruiting labor—both men and women. Research by Dag Andreassen shows that it was particularly hard to fill the position of fillet cutter, traditionally a woman's job. Frequent advertisements were placed in various newspapers in northern Norway. In 1943 alone, a dozen similar ads appeared in *Harstad Tidende*, such as: "Female laborers are needed at our fillet factory for the winter season 1944. Piecework. Free travel."

At full operation, the fillet factory in Melbu required around 300 workers and salaried employees. Many fillet cutters were needed—a process that, as in Hammerfest and Langstranda, was partly done by hand and considered women's work. During the high season, thirty women were required per shift, with three shifts in the working day. Additionally, there was a need for thirty-one women and fifteen men in the packing department, ten dock workers, one warehouse supervisor, and around twenty laborers for various tasks such as carpentry (e.g., building boxes) and maintenance. There were also machinists, general laborers, foremen, and inspectors. A persistent labor shortage was recorded, with a particular shortage of female laborers. By 1944, men had to be employed for fillet work. This led to higher labor costs because women were paid less than men. (Equal pay for equal work was not introduced in Norway until the late 1960s.)

Andreassen notes that the reason for the difficulty in recruiting women for the Melbu plant remains unclear. The Vesterålen Archipelago was dotted with small farms where women were often busy managing cows and sheep and raising children, although some still took filleting jobs. Their husbands were fishermen, and many families managed well during the wartime boom without needing to sell labor to the factory. However, the Melbu fillet factory may also have been unpopular for other reasons. This was likely not solely because it was a "German plant": people were more willing to work at other German-run facilities in the area. Rather, Gunnar Fredriksen's personality may have deterred locals. He was a member of Nasjonal Samling (the Norwegian Nazi Party) and served as Germany's vice consul for Lofoten and Vesterålen during the war. Working for a prominent Norwegian Nazi may have been considered worse than working directly for the Germans.

Soviet prisoners of war were held on the island of Haugøya, about three kilometers from Fredriksen's frozen fillet factory. The prisoners built a fortress there, intended in part to protect the factory. However, no "eastern women" were brought to work at Melbu, even though the management expressed interest in accepting women from Hammerfest after the evacuation in autumn 1944.

In addition to labor shortages, Melbu also struggled with high levels of absenteeism, which management suspected was due to workers leaving under false pretenses. One contributing factor was that many laborers had additional duties on local farms and would leave the factory when their farms required attention. The absentee problem diminished somewhat when management introduced "leave-of-absence" privileges during spring planting and hay harvesting seasons. However, many workers failed to return after their leave, further compromising the factory's production. As a result, much of the fish spoiled and was lost.

The German Chief Engineer, Ferdinand Flor, complained to the SD intelligence service that getting Director Gunnar Fredriksen to act on the ongoing labor difficulties caused him endless trouble. High-level positions in factories, such as the one held by Flor, were invariably filled by Germans, as Norway lacked the necessary expertise. Flor sent numerous reports regarding absenteeism due to illness. Some absences were due to demonstrable illnesses and accidents. For example, female fillet cutters often sliced themselves and suffered from infected fingers. During the busiest month in the factory's history, March 1944, Fredriksen reported that they had to plan for an absenteeism rate of up to 20 percent among the fish-cutters. The high rate of illness and accidents was met with suspicion. The authorities were never able to determine whether the workers were genuinely sick or engaged in acts of sabotage. Engineer Flor supported the latter theory and reported his concerns to the security services.

The imposition of tighter control by the SD intelligence service in 1943 arose from allegations of sabotage. There had been tampering with packing and weighing processes, as well as issues with the aging, motor-driven refrigeration system. All of these problems were attributed to sabotage. The plant was frequently visited by representatives of the German authorities, including security services from Narvik, Bodø, and Svolvær, as well as officials from the Reichskommissariat branch in Bodø.

In 1944, control was further intensified after a crate of spoiled fish arrived in Hamburg. Someone had expressed their feelings about Norwegian fish being sent to the enemy by using the crate as a toilet. Following this incident, German personnel were employed to verify employees' identification papers, and the SD placed at least one informer at the plant.

13

MARFA: WORK, RESISTANCE, AND LOVE

We have already described Galina Korolenko's abduction from the Russian countryside, and the great black hole of information that for years shrouded her and Fedor's arrival and life in Norway, where Yuri was born. Yuri recalls a few facts from that period in his life, including the pain his mother continued to feel in her hands for the rest of her life—the result of working with ice-cold water on the conveyor belts that brought in fish for filleting. He also remembers her telling him that she and other prisoners would sometimes walk down to the seashore and gaze into the distance for a long time. "Gloomy landscape, stones, ruins, and cold winds," he comments. "They really longed to go home." But when Galina died in 1992, she had never spoken to Yuri in any depth about her time in captivity.

Fortunately for the writing of this book, that is not the case for other women who survived into old age with sharp memories.

Marija "Marfa" Maksimovna Stepina was abducted in Bryansk Oblast—one of thirty-four children whose mothers were taken from districts in southwestern Russia, bordering on Ukraine. Born in a village near Smolensk, a small but historic city about 300 kilometers west of Moscow, Marfa was fourteen and living near the city of Bryansk when Nazi forces attacked the Soviet Union in August 1941.

She left a detailed description of her abduction in an interview with her daughter Valentina:

In 1941, my mother's family, my father and sister lived in the village of Sinezyorki, which was occupied by the Germans who came to the house along with the local police. How could I protect myself? If you had relatives or friends in the police force, you were not taken away. The Germans and the police gave the orders to get ready to deliver me to the railroad station. There were many people from the nearest village there. I knew women from the villages of Butrjo and Lbi for instance. This was not about volunteering. Everyone was committed to their land. There was a strong tie between relatives. We were loaded into freight cars. During the loading, a "corridor" was created by Germans and local police. We were transported to Bryansk. There we were quartered in a school. After a while we were transported to Poland, then to Denmark and Norway. We went to Norway by boat.

Her memories describe a demanding daily routine at the factory:

We worked from eight in the morning to six in the evening, sixty hours a week. We washed the raw fish and packed it down in big boxes, nine kilos (20 lb.) to every box. It was cold work because of the cold water and because it was cold in the room where we worked. There was a draft through the premises that we felt inside the factory. We stood on a platform above the floor. The ice-cold water ran under our feet. Our hands were so frozen that the fish stuck to them. I packed quickly to stay warm.

Rumors of sabotage created doubt and suspicion between the women on the production line:

The other girls were grumpy and asked why I worked so hard. They wanted to work slowly so that the fish would rot. But when you worked fast it got a little warmer. We got rubber gloves, but our hands only froze even more.

Despite being a hard worker, she was regarded as uncooperative by the Germans. She remembered coworkers encouraging "go-slow actions," and that those who took part—or were accused of other forms of sabotage—had their names tattooed on their arms. Marfa bore such a tattoo, still distinct on the near-transparent skin of her left arm.

She also describes the brutality of the various capos at the plant. Workers were kicked and beaten, both at the plant and in the camp, as depicted in the prisoner Dmitrij's drawings.

In one respect, however, the forced laborers at Frostfilet were better off than prisoners in other camps: they were not intentionally starved or worked to death. They were adequately clothed and had access to fish, which they found ways to prepare on the factory premises. They also managed to obtain cod-liver oil and other fish by-products. Marfa recalled that they secretly took milt from the factory and cooked it on the wood-burning stoves in the barracks.

Love and Its Consequences

Marfa Stepina with fellow prisoner Arkady Mozerin in 1945. (Photo: Valentina Stepina.)

We have only one photograph of Marfa from her years in Norway, taken at Langstranda in the spring of 1945—probably after Norway was liberated in May, and not long before she returned to Russia. Similar photographs have been found in Russia, though it is likely they were taken by Norwegians, as copies also appear in albums owned by people in the Bodø area. In the photo, she stands with Arkady Mozerin, a fellow prisoner. Clad in a long coat and heavy boots, Marfa appears as a round-faced, robust young woman with a bright smile. In contrast, Arkady wears street shoes and a vest, and looks warily at the camera from under a black cap.

We know almost nothing about the relationship of Marfa and Arkady during their time at Langstranda. However, we do know that it resulted in the birth of their daughter, Valentina, while they were still in Norway (see chapter 19).

Because the male and female forced laborers lived separately, in quarters divided by barbed wire, opportunities to meet with any degree of privacy were rare. Yet photographs from these years include sketches of loving couples encircled by hearts, chiseled into the walls of the sorting and filleting stations at the factory. One of the drawings is signed and dated April 21, 1941, suggesting it was made during the major construction period at the factory.

Like other couples, Marfa and Arkady may have found secret meeting places in the factory where they could be intimate or managed to get through the barbed-wire fences. Later on, as the tide of war turned, conditions became less restrictive, and there were more opportunities for couples to meet and even visit the nearby town.

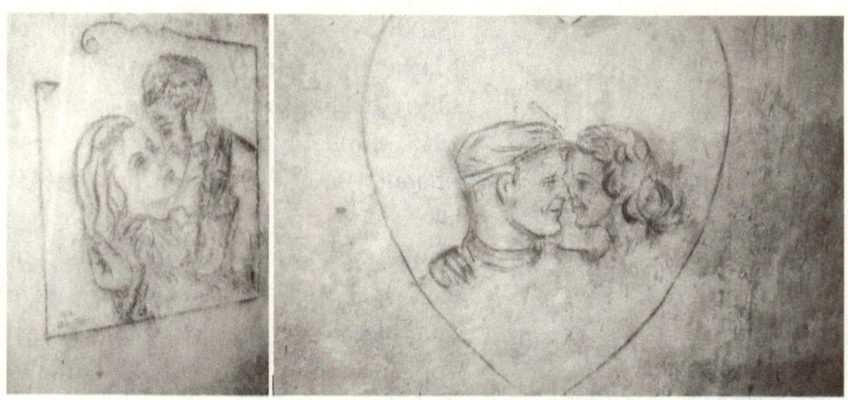

Two drawings of couples made in fresh cement in the factory. (Photo: Karl Erik Brekke.)

The children of these relationships may have been born in the barracks or in the prison camp field hospital. There may have been experienced women among the older laborers who could assist during childbirth. More complicated cases may have been transferred to Bodø Hospital, although this is speculative, as there is no official registration of these births in 1944–45. The wartime records of Bodø Hospital did not survive. However, another document from 1945 shows that among the children born at Langstranda to women prisoners during this period, only one—Jonni, the son of Hanna Koljada, whose story is recounted later in chapter 19—was listed as having a Norwegian father; the rest of the fathers were listed as Soviet citizens. One child listed a German father, Hans.

Frostfilet permanently employed a German doctor. A telegram dated September 12, 1942, from the County Commissioner of Nordland to the Health Department at the Interior Ministry in Oslo, emphasized that the presence of Soviet workers warranted a full-time German doctor on staff. Childbirth was not the only reason a medical officer was needed: the plant required a healthy workforce to maintain production. The machinery posed many risks, and it was important to treat accidents quickly. Records show that prisoners received treatment both at Bodø Hospital and from the local surgeon, Dr. Anton Johnson, a much-respected figure whose story will be related in further detail later.

A Love Affair with a Sad Ending

A Russian soldier, Vladimir Kozlov, arrived at the fish factory around May or June 1942. He was one of the few who managed to escape and get back to the Soviet Union.

Like Dimitrij, he was transferred to the roadwork project at Fauske. Vladimir fell ill and was admitted to the hospital in Bodø, where he met the nurse Gunvor Galtung Haavik. She spoke Russian and was interested in Russian culture. A passionate love affair developed between them.

Gunvor's later life was deeply influenced by this relationship. Vladimir Kozlov was not simply involved with Gunvor—he was also obsessed with the idea of escape and asked for her help. The opportunity arose in August 1944 while he was working at the munitions factory at Klungset near Fauske. There he met a Norwegian, Magnus Nordvik, who devised an escape plan. At the Nordvik family farm, clothes and provisions were prepared for a journey across the mountains to unoccupied Sweden, and Gunvor gave Vladimir a Silva compass. Two other prisoners joined the escape. The escapees walked about 150 kilometers, past Sulitjelma to the Indigenous Sámi village of

Mavas on the Swedish side of the border. There, they reported to the police in Arjeplog in northern Sweden and were sent by train to the Lisma camp south of Stockholm.

In 1944, there were nine hundred Soviet prisoners in Sweden who had managed to escape from Norway and Finland. The Soviet embassy in Stockholm, headed by Alexandra Kollontai, handled the repatriation of these 900 Soviet citizens. Kollontai was a pioneer of women's rights and served as the Bolsheviks' first female cabinet minister in 1920. She headed the consular service in Norway during the 1920s and later played an important role as the Soviet ambassador in what was called "The Casablanca of the North"—Stockholm—during the war.

As said before, after Nazi Germany's attack on the Soviet Union on June 22, 1941, Finland joined the Axis on June 25. This alliance ended on September 19, 1944, with the Moscow Armistice. Three days later, on September 22, 1944, Swedish authorities approved the repatriation plan. It was decided that two steamships, the *Ørnen* and *Varjo,* would transport the Soviets to the port of Turku in Finland, which by then had withdrawn from the war. From there, the escapees were sent by train to Leningrad, where the three-year-long blockade had been broken.

Vladimir Kozlov returned to his homeland and later began working for the KGB. This would eventually have serious consequences for Gunvor Galtung Haavik, who never forgot him. She became a translator during the liberation of northern Norway and was later employed by the Norwegian Foreign Ministry. She was stationed in Moscow for several years as a secretary. There, she managed to reconnect with Vladimir, and after rekindling their relationship, she was coerced into becoming an active spy for the USSR, continuing her espionage after returning to Norway.

Gunvor was arrested in Oslo in January 1977 while meeting with KGB agent Alexander Prinzipalov. The first Norwegian woman to be arrested for spying for the Soviet Union, she died of a heart attack while being held in Drammen District Prison before her trial.

Her story is the subject of both a novel, *Iskyss* (*The Ice Kiss*) by Alf R. Jacobsen, and a feature film of the same name by Knut Erik Jensen.

14

ANNY: THE GIRL WHO STAYED

On June 22, 1942, the German cargo ship *Levante* arrived in Hammerfest with several hundred Soviet prisoners of war on board. The roster included 150 young women from the German-occupied parts of Eastern Europe.

Among them was seventeen-year-old Hanna Koljada from Dnipropetrovsk in Ukraine, who had been abducted by the German army straight from her school desk. Unlike the others, however, she remained in Hammerfest after the war and became a Norwegian citizen.

Now known by her Norwegian name, Anny Evensen, she was ninety-three years old when we interviewed her in Hammerfest on May 29 and 30, 2017—almost seventy-five years to the day since her journey to Hammerfest began in Ukraine. On the spring day of the interview, snow was in the air, and a fierce northwesterly wind swept in from the Arctic Ocean. But Anny was accustomed to Hammerfest's wind and bad weather. She maintained that she had not missed her homeland. She had visited her sister in Ukraine in 1974 and 1982, but had not been able to return to her birthplace. As a Norwegian citizen, she was considered a foreigner. At the time, the city of Dnipropetrovsk was closed to foreigners for security reasons, like many cities during the Cold War, especially those involved in weapons manufacturing or military research. Weapons are still manufactured in Dnipropetrovsk today.

Anny was, however, able to open her Norwegian home to visitors from Ukraine. Her mother, sister, and other relatives visited her over the years. She died at the age of 98 in 2022.

Anny Evensen in 2017. (Photo: Liv Mjelde.)

Her house on Skiveien had a magnificent view over Hammerfest. It was the house she and her husband, Jacob Evensen, built after the war, and where three of her four children were born. Jonni, the child she had at Langstranda in 1945, drowned at the age of six in Lake Storvannet, not far from the house. From her home, Anny could look out at Fuglenes (Bird Point) and Støttabakken (Statue Hill), where she and many other young women had been housed in the barracks on the outskirts of Hammerfest. Fuglenes takes its name from the headland where birds have come to rest year after year during their migratory spring flights from milder climates: starlings, snow buntings, seagulls, terns, crows, and magpies. The birds arrived of their own free will—unlike the young women who came aboard the *Levante* in 1942.

Taken and Transported

Anny was born on October 7, 1924, in the village of Karkenskoiei. She tells of a difficult time and much poverty growing up. Her mother, Jefrosinia Koljada, was widowed at the age of thirty-two and became the sole provider for three children. Trained as a seamstress, she was able to earn some money for their upkeep, keeping hunger at bay with the vegetables she grew on a small plot of land, relying particularly on potatoes.

Anny still remembers how, on May 31, 1942, she and two schoolmates were taken directly from their school to the railroad station.

Hanna's mother had heard rumors of what was happening and rushed to the station with a suitcase of food and clothing. Thus began an exhausting three-week journey: first by train to Stettin on the Polish coast, and then onward by boat, crammed into the hold of the ship *Levante* alongside male Soviet prisoners of war. The female prisoners were between 15 and 40 years old. Anny was 17.

The young women had no idea where they were being taken. Accustomed to their own vast, often landlocked countries, many had never seen the sea before they found themselves aboard a ship following the wild, rocky Norwegian coastline.

The daily run between Bergen and Kirkenes by *Hurtigruten*, the coastal ferry service, has provided a lifeline to the people of the north for more than a hundred years, and continued to do so during the war. For centuries, people had settled along this coastline and endured a tough existence as fishers and farmers. The coastal steamers transported people and goods, as well as mail and news—often delivered by word of mouth—to the many settlements along Norway's extensive coast. During the war, the ferry service moved to the front line. The sea here is often rough, with wind and stormy weather, and those were particularly dangerous times. German-controlled ships were frequent targets for Allied submarines, and the coast was heavily land-mined. Fourteen ships were sunk during the war, resulting in the loss of 700 lives. In one of the worst incidents, ninety Norwegian passengers, fifty crew members, and more than 300 German soldiers died when the steamship *Prinsesse Ragnhild* sank outside Bodø on October 23, 1940, likely after hitting a mine.

Anny recalled the journey on the *Levante* as interminable:

> *We were separated from the Russian male prisoners. We were not allowed to talk to them. We generally had to stay below decks. We were barely allowed on deck for a little fresh air. Finally, after three weeks of travel, we reached the harbor. We had no idea where in the world we were. We had never seen the sea, and unlike the mountains we had seen on our journey and in Hammerfest, the mountains were now all around us.*

Arrival

When the ship finally arrived at Hammerfest, the women were billeted in barracks at Fuglenes. The citizens of Hammerfest had seen the Germans installing barracks enclosed by barbed-wire fencing not far from the Lohmann factory. The barracks were built to house this imported workforce. *Finnmark Folkeblad* published the following notice on June 23, 1942: "Some Ukrainian women are coming to work at the fillet factory. All private dealings with them are forbidden."

The women were forced to begin work from their very first day, taking their places in fish-filleting production with the Hamburg-based company Vereinigte Tiefkühlgesellschaft Lohmann & Co. (VERTILO).

By this time, the frozen fillet factory at Fuglenes had been in operation for almost a year and a half. As we have seen, the Germans' attempt to force Norwegian women into filleting work and "other socially important tasks" had failed; production quotas in Hammerfest had not been met. Over time, more young women arrived from the East, and by 1944 perhaps as many as four hundred Soviet women made up Germany's captive labor force in Hammerfest. These women had been seized from various locations and were of different ages, ranging from early teens to some in their fifties and sixties. Some had been taken straight from school, like Anny, while others had worked as shoemakers or engineers.

The researcher Bjørn-Petter Finstad refers to these women as the pioneers of Norway's frozen fish industry, owing to their role in operating new freezing technology. Especially in Germany and the United States, the production of fresh fish had found new forms that were changing both production methods and consumption habits. Norway had been experimenting with machinery and cooperating internationally to enter this market in the decades leading up to the war, but real success did not come until the wartime period.

Thor Thorsen (2000) wrote in an article years later: "I remember the painful and somber atmosphere among Hammerfest's citizens as they witnessed the human cargo of more than a hundred women who came with the steamship Levante. Young girls around fourteen or fifteen years old came with their little bundles of hand luggage." Thor was fifteen when his father, Wessel Thorsen, was ordered by the authorities to move to Hammerfest from Vardø as part of "the national work effort" and take up a job at the Lohmann factory. Thor still had a year left of school when he came to Hammerfest, completing his final year of mandatory education while working part-time at the factory.

The women were housed in barracks near the filleting factory. Each room held ten to twelve women, who slept in bunks on straw mattresses. They were issued coats, dresses, and scarves. A directive from Berlin required that workers from the East wear the capital letter O (for *Ostarbeiterinnen*) on their chest or sleeve. Alf Jacobsen recalled that the women also had to wear a piece of cloth with the inscription *"Freien nach Osten"* ("Free from the East") on their backs—reflecting the Nazi claim that the workers had been liberated from what they called the "barbarous East."

Upon arrival in Hammerfest, the women were subjected to medical examinations and delousing at the hospital. Dr. Christian Spiering served as chief medical officer for both the German battalion and the citizens of Hammerfest from June 1942 to March 1944. He was responsible for the health of both the Norwegian workforce and the Soviet women at the Lohmann factory. The young women had arrived in the cold north wearing summer dresses and flimsy shoes, so his first responsibility was to ensure they had warm clothing and solid footwear suitable for working in the factory.

Dr. Spiering reported that of those who arrived in June 1942, three were already pregnant. On October 23, 1942, he wrote a recommendation stating that ten women needed to be sent to Germany or back to Ukraine for medical reasons, including two pregnant women. The first births took place in Hammerfest in January and March 1943. Anny believed that one of the women had a relationship with a German guard during the voyage. She also recalled that the Wehrmacht had threatened to take the children away, but this did not happen.

However, the health issues faced by the women were not only physical. They were accustomed to a completely different natural environment: Ukraine, with its wide, flat steppes and warm summer nights. Now they were in Hammerfest, one of the world's northernmost towns, where the midnight sun is a perpetual presence in June.

Hammerfest is exposed to the northern sea and winds that seem to blow directly from the nearby North Pole. The weather is harsh and can change in an instant, even in summer. Anny recounted that some of the women couldn't handle the transition. They became disoriented and mentally unbalanced, and had to be sent south.

Some traces of these cases can be found in archival records. For example, in a letter from the Wehrmacht to an official named Wachs in the Labor and Social Services Department in Oslo, we found that female workers from the East were sent from Hammerfest to Tromsø on January 16, 1943. They were expected to arrive in Hamburg around January 25. A message from the German Regional Inspector Bremer in Tromsø, dated March 30, 1943, concerned the forwarding of twenty-six letters addressed to the "Ukrainian women." These women had been placed in the Neumünster camp in the District of Nordmark in Germany. The letters were forwarded from Hamburg to the camp on April 16, 1943. All the women were sent to camps and put to work in Germany.

Working Conditions

Accessing information about everyday life during the war years in Hammerfest proved challenging. We were fortunate that Anny opened her door to us and shared some of her memories. She became a forewoman responsible for timecards and for keeping everything in her department in order. She attributed her position to her ability to speak German, which allowed her to serve as a link between the bosses and the female filleting workers.

It was also fortunate that Thor Thorsen had recorded his memories of working at the Lohmann factory with the *russefangene* (the "Russian prisoners," as the Soviet women were commonly called in Hammerfest, regardless of nationality). He recalled that the women prisoners participated in most work operations alongside the Norwegians. He primarily worked with the young women, often doing cleaning tasks. As noted previously, hygiene was essential, and the factory had to be thoroughly cleaned every day. The women had to scrub the six freezer units by hand, removing ice, salt, and freezer liquids. It was tough, hard, and uncomfortable work.

The women walked to and from work each day under the watch of German guards. Production took place in two shifts: from 6:00 to 15:00, and from 15:00 to 23:00. Shifts changed weekly, so the women alternated between morning and evening shifts. The uneven supply of raw materials naturally affected production at all the frozen fillet factories, with varying demands at different times. When supplies ran low in Hammerfest, the women were assigned to other tasks, such as working at the navy warehouse or cleaning the Grand Hotel, where many Germans were quartered. When fish and production materials were sufficient, they worked around the clock.

In addition to the specialized job of filleting, the women also performed tasks traditionally considered men's work. Fishing vessels from Hammerfest collected fish from various small villages along the coast of North Troms and East Finnmark and brought the catch to the factory docks. When the boats arrived, crews unloaded the fish onto the dock, and some women were included in these work crews. The fish was then transported directly to the production areas, where other women handled the filleting and, after freezing, the packing. The finished products were loaded onto Dutch and German cargo vessels and shipped to Germany.

Among his recollections, Thor described a dramatic incident that took place at the harbor. A worker named Holger Johansen was the "boss" there—one of the few Norwegians in a supervisory position in which his ability to speak German had played a large role. On a June day, one of the women fell into the sea, and a call for help rang out. Holger, a strong swimmer, immediately tore off his clothes and boots and jumped into the icy water. The woman, strong and panicking, struggled in the freezing sea. Holger slapped her to calm her down and then managed to drag her to shore, where many helping hands pulled them out and wrapped them in warm clothing. Holger later remarked with some surprise that he found his boots still waiting for him.

Anny recalled that, in dealing with the cold, it helped to put one's hand into the fish liver: when the fingertips began to warm, one could feel confident of being protected from frostbite that day. Still, Dr. Spiering had to treat many hand injuries, as well as bronchial infections, rheumatism, and hereditary diseases. He noted that the women were driven hard because production was regarded as crucial to the German food supply. He wrote of his efforts to protect the women, and often had to intervene on their behalf to improve their conditions. His diary notes record that he was summoned before the Gestapo and the German factory management on the charge that his treatment of the Soviet women was too humane.

15

DAILY LIFE AND A STRIKE

When they were not working, the women for the most part stayed indoors. Comings and goings at the camp were forbidden, but the prohibition was not strictly enforced. Many of the women would sneak out along the shore whenever they saw an opportunity. If they were caught, their punishment was to empty the outdoor privies.

The city was blacked out; there were no streetlights. It was often cold and dark. People lived for long periods in gloom, alleviated only by the white snow. The harsh climate and the dank winter nights were difficult for those not accustomed to such conditions. A rudimentary central heating system did, however, provide a tolerable temperature in the barrack rooms. The women were allowed to write letters home, and sometimes they received letters and packages. The food they were served was simple, consisting of fish with turnips and fishmeal bread. Occasionally, they had smoked haddock and dried fish provided by the inhabitants of Hammerfest. In general, however, there was too little food. There was also a shortage of clothing. Most of the women wore work aprons and rubber boots—items Dr. Spiering had negotiated for to protect their feet. Outside the factory, they wore street shoes.

However, Anny also recalled that the women in Hammerfest did not accept just anything. During their first winter, they organized an action that may have had no equivalent among female prisoners in war-torn Norway. Due to the poor food and cold living quarters, they went on strike and refused to work. The barracks were surrounded by German soldiers and officers, accompanied by intimidating German shepherd dogs trying to force them outside. The women remained unfazed. They held their ground, with 100 percent of the women participating in the strike. They stood together in the barracks, packed tightly like herring in a barrel, singing songs of lament that echoed across the city.

To the great surprise of Hammerfest's inhabitants, something remarkable happened: the women succeeded. They obtained better food and warmer clothing. In the barracks, they received a daily loaf of fishmeal bread to share among four women, along with a little butter and some jam. At the factory, they also began receiving a meal of cooked fish in the middle of the day.

It was often difficult to be so far from home. But the good relations between the Soviet women and the local Hammerfest population made their lives a bit easier. Acquaintances and friendships were formed through work at the factory and during the times when the women snuck into town. The filleting workers were easily identifiable by their simple coats, headscarves, and the label "O" on their arms. People in Hammerfest recall the brown clothing they wore when they were marched with German guards to the cinema. Anny remembered attaching snaps to hers, so she could easily remove and reattach the label.

Sexual Relations, Official and Un-official

Throughout Europe, sexual relations between prisoners and local inhabitants were a many-sided problem for the Wehrmacht. Anny recalls that the women were popular among the male inhabitants of Hammerfest. Many of them had sweethearts, as she herself did.

In fact, archival records show that the women at the Lohmann factory were of particular concern to the Nazis. The SS doctors overseeing them were disturbed by their relationships with men. A report dated February 8, 1944, shows that a concerned SS Captain, Dr. Riel, wrote to the authorities in Oslo:

> *In Hammerfest there is a fish factory which, among other things, employs female Ukrainians. These are housed in a camp. The navy's crew, stationed in the city, is forbidden from having any relations with the Ukrainian women. Experience has shown that this restriction can only be enforced with the utmost difficulty. The commandant is said to have considered lifting the restriction. In spite of severe punishment, offenses continue to occur.*

The Nazis had issued a general prohibition against sexual relations between Germans and forced laborers, but to no avail. Dr. Riel continued:

> *The Ukrainian women have declared that they cannot understand why the soldiers are denied relations with them. In Ukraine, a certain amount of contact is permitted between both officers and soldiers and the local population. Officers moved from the Eastern Front to northern Norway also find the restriction incomprehensible.*

There were many young soldiers in Hammerfest. The town and surrounding islands were heavily fortified, with significant German military installations. Large numbers of soldiers guarded areas such as Melkøya, Elvetun, and Kvalfjord, which was considered a potential Allied landing site. Hammerfest was also an important U-boat base for operations in the Barents Sea. As a result, there was a high concentration of servicemen who had limited opportunities to seek physical companionship elsewhere.

Dr. Riel wrote that because submarine crews endured long patrols in confined quarters with little opportunity for physical activity:

> *It [...] seems appropriate, because of the untenable relations with the Ukrainian women, that a brothel should be established in Hammerfest.*

Dr. Paris at the Reichskommissariat in Oslo, however, took a more pragmatic stance, likely resulting in Dr. Riel's suggestion being set aside:

> *I am personally of the opinion that in this regard no difficulties should be made for the soldiers. But establishing a brothel up there is impossible.*

To put this into a wider context: brothels were, in fact, established across Norway to serve the occupation forces. German women worked in a military brothel in Oslo as early as the autumn of 1940. Dr. Spiering cared for these women in his first job in Norway before being assigned to Hammerfest. The brothel, called Haus Sphinx, was located at 6 Dronningens Street in central Oslo and remained there until the end of the war. It was a French-style officers' brothel staffed by French women and a German hostess, open daily from 4 p.m. to 11 p.m. Organisation Todt had its offices in the same building.

Holms Hotel in Geilo, a small mountain town between Oslo and Bergen, also hosted a brothel that housed French prostitutes. In the north, there were also so-called "floating brothels" that trafficked German, French, and Belgian *Einsatzfrauen* ("national war effort women") who serviced soldiers. A brothel in Lakselv, not far from Hammerfest, was staffed by Norwegian women from Oslo and Bergen. Their clientele consisted of minor German officers and soldiers en route to battlegrounds around Lista and Petsamo.

The topic of these "houses of pleasure" remained taboo across Scandinavia until recently.

Following the end of the war, women who had sexual relations with German men faced immense hardship (see also chapter 6). They were persecuted, maltreated, and imprisoned across Europe. Their hair was cut off, and they were ostracized from their communities. Often young and unaware of the larger context of the war, they were open to romance and sexual relationships, blind to the possible consequences.

There is little concrete information about the specific situation in Hammerfest regarding Norwegian women's relationships with the German soldiers who surrounded them in daily life. Male prisoners from the USSR were also present in nearby camps, but there has been little willingness to discuss those interactions.

In fact, accessing information about everyday life during the war years in Hammerfest proved very difficult, although Anny willingly shared her story. The archives were closed when we visited, and the researchers at the museum center were not eager to share their knowledge. Most of our information comes from other archives and documents provided by other researchers.

We found correspondence in the Trondheim archives that confirmed the SS doctor in Oslo was concerned about the "Ukrainian women," likely for racist reasons. As Slavs, they were viewed as a threat to the purity of Aryan blood. This obsession with racial purity was a long-standing concern for the Nazis. After coming to power in 1933, any advertising or public mention of condoms was made punishable by law. German women were expected to bear as many Aryan children as possible. Adolf Hitler even spoke of waging a "minor war" on condoms.

Discussion around contraceptives was forbidden not only in Germany during the interwar period but also in Norway, where it remained illegal to advertise contraceptives until 1939. However, World War II complicated the issue. Nazi policymakers found themselves struggling to reconcile race ideology with pragmatic concerns. In 1942 the Reich's Minister of Health, Leonardo Conti, emphasized supplying condoms to German soldiers in Soviet occupied areas to prevent Slavic women from giving birth to "impure bastards."

Anny Returns to Hammerfest

On May 31, three years to the day since she had been abducted from her school in the Ukraine, Anny and Jacob married. Years later, in her interview, Anny recalled the wedding: held in a Norwegian pastor's office in Bodin, her bridesmaid a girlfriend from the Ukraine, whilst a local man, Johnny Larsen, was Jacob's best man.

In 1946, after spending a year in an evacuation camp at Harstad, the family traveled back to Hammerfest, which had been destroyed in the Nazis' scorched-earth withdrawal. More time in temporary barracks awaited them there.

Anny spent a total of thirteen years in various barracks, first when she worked at the filleting factory and later during the long years of reconstruction. She was the only one of the forced laborers to return to Hammerfest. She later received restitution from Germany in the form of 21,000 kroner for having worked in the fishing industry at Hammerfest, Svinøya and Langstranda from June 6, 1942, to May 8, 1945. The head of the Hammerfest Historical Association, Arnulf Olsen, and Roland Masslich, from Cuxhaven, helped her compose the application.

PART IV

THE TIDE TURNS

16

FINNMARK ON FIRE

In late October 1944, women laborers from the Lohmann factory in Hammerfest were loaded onto fishing vessels and sent to the town of Svolvær, about 800 kilometers to the southwest. Before continuing this part of the women's story, it is important to place it in a wider context.

The tides of war had turned over the previous two years, and the liberation of Norway was underway. After the dark years of advances by the seemingly unstoppable Wehrmacht, the Allies had begun to make progress on several fronts. Across the Mediterranean, the triumph at El Alamein on November 11, 1942, led to the capitulation of the German and Italian armies in North Africa in May 1943. In the Pacific, the Battle of Midway, fought from June 4 to 7, 1942, marked the first major defeat of the Japanese Imperial Navy by American forces—and the beginning of a campaign that would culminate in the dropping of two atomic bombs on Hiroshima and Nagasaki.

Closer to Norway, the surrender of the German Sixth Army at Stalingrad on February 2, 1943, marked a decisive turning point in the war. With the defeat of the Axis forces—including not only German but also Croatian, Italian, Hungarian, and Romanian troops—the Red Army had halted the Nazi advance into the Soviet Union. The losses on both sides were enormous. The Battle of Stalingrad is regarded as one of the bloodiest in history, with an estimated 1.5 million people perishing over the course of 199 days of fighting. Photographs of the city in 1943 show that only one building remained standing.

Center of Stalingrad after liberation, 1943 (Wikimedia Commons, RIA Novosti)

The suffering and sacrifice endured by both soldiers and civilians left an indelible mark on the collective memory of the former Soviet Union and on Allied nations across Europe. Even today, that legacy resonates. In the northern arrondissements of Paris, passengers on the Metro are reminded of the battle as the train stops at Stalingrad Station.

Renamed Volgograd in 1961 during the process of de-Stalinization, the city remains a powerful symbol of the battle. A massive memorial complex, crowned by the 52-meter-high sculpture *The Motherland Calls,* stands on the Mamayev Kurgan heights above the city. The heroic victory was recognized outside the Soviet Union as well. Britain's King George VI awarded the citizens of Stalingrad a jewel-encrusted longsword, known as the "Sword of Stalingrad," to commemorate their perseverance and bravery in battle.

Chapter 16

The Miracle of Litsa

In comparison with the titanic scale of these battles, Hitler's first major defeat on the Eastern front—termed the "Miracle of Litsa" by the writer Alf Jacobsen—is much less renowned. At precisely 2:30 a.m. on June 22, 1941, the northernmost component of Operation Barbarossa, the Nazis' invasion of the Soviet Union, began from Kirkenes, about 400 kilometers east of Hammerfest. From its staging point there, the Mountain Corps Norway (Gebirgskorps Norwegen) under General Eduard Dietl began its march, heading towards the border at the village of Boris Gleb at the Eastern Front's most northerly point, while a second force moved up from northern Finland. The ultimate goal was to capture the Soviet port of Murmansk. The port was vital for the wartime supply of arms into the Soviet Union by Allied ships, which sailed along the Norwegian coast in the so-called Murmansk Run. The port city was also the deployment point for thousands of men and women who were defending their homeland in the north.

The Nazis never reached Murmansk; their offensive came to a brutal halt in the rugged terrain along the Litsa River. Fierce fighting between German and Soviet forces in the first weeks of the campaign settled into a bloody stalemate that lasted for three years. Nature is an unpredictable force in war and often plays games with generals. The soldiers of the Red Army were not the only ones to assault the invading forces: massive battalions of mosquitoes attacked relentlessly all summer, and in the seemingly endless winter months, the soldiers had to contend with bitter cold, deep snow, and storms. An estimated fifty to seventy thousand soldiers from both sides lost their lives, but Nazi forces were never able to cross the Litsa River or conquer Murmansk.

From 1944 onward, the Allies were advancing across Europe and the USSR. On October 22, Soviet forces crossed the Jakob's River, the border between Russia and Norway, and swiftly approached Kirkenes. Approximately 113,000 Soviet soldiers took part in the attack on the German Nineteenth Army in northern Norway over the following weeks.

The Women of the Red Army

Men were, however, not the only ones who came marching across the border.

Soviet women had been eager to join the army when Nazi Germany attacked. Crowds of women stood in line outside recruiting offices all over the Soviet Union in the days following June 22, 1941. They wanted to fight on an equal footing with the men. One million Soviet women served in all branches of the Soviet armed forces during World War II. They were bomber and fighter pilots; they fought at Leningrad and Stalingrad.

The most notorious bomber regiment was known as the "Night Witches," owing to the unique bombing style of its pilots. They idled their engines near their targets and glided to the bomb-release point, meaning only the noise of the wind announced their presence. Nazi soldiers likened the sound to witches on broomsticks, giving rise to the nickname. Women also participated in guerrilla activity in the cities and in the partisan wars throughout the occupied areas of the Soviet Union. The bravery and fortitude of these women were little known at the time or in the years following the war.

In Norway, a female battalion was also part of the Soviet forces. This aspect of the war remained little known to most Norwegians until 2006, when Anne Helskog's eyewitness account *Det er bombevær i natt. Fem år i Festung Kirkenes* (*Tonight Is Good Bombing Weather: Five Years in Fortress Kirkenes*) was published. Anne lived in Kirkenes during the war, and her diary entries describe in detail everyday life there between May 4, 1940, and May 17, 1945. The typewritten diary had been forgotten after the war but was found years later by her granddaughter, Tone Helskog, in a drawer. Tone had it published in 2006.

This little book provides insight into buried knowledge from the war, including the fact that Anne saw many women in the Red Army. In fact, she observed an entire female division soon after the town was liberated: "Stalwart, strong, and fearless, that's how they seemed. High praise and many stories are circulating about their bravery in the field. It is said that they in no way are inferior to the men." She continues her description of the female Soviet soldiers as she had observed them on October 31:

> *"They certainly fully share the hardships of camp life with their male counterparts. Yesterday afternoon I saw some of them sitting on the ground down by the stream, fixing their hair. They were naked to the waist and washing their bodies. It looked as if they were having a very good time with the ice-cold water and the nice winter air."*

The soldiers slept out of doors. Those who did not have a tent—and there were many who didn't—made tents from rags and crept inside at nightfall. It is cold weather in the north in the winter.

The German Retreat

Weeks before the Soviet arrival in the town, the Germans began to prepare their retreat from Kirkenes. The order was given to start Operation Nordlicht, using scorched-earth tactics. Every building was to be burned down, and all domestic animals killed, to deny the enemy all forms of infrastructure created by human effort and ingenuity. Nothing was to be left behind for the Bolsheviks.

The first "Retreat-cars" appeared in the streets. These cars had an "R" painted on the front and rear windshields, indicating a retreat down the road to the south. Norway's Quisling government was directly involved in these plans. On October 11, two Nasjonal Samling ministers, Jonas Lie and Johan Lippestad, arrived in Kirkenes, but they immediately had to seek protection in a bomb shelter alongside the local population. The Allies attacked Kirkenes around noon. Four large ships were attacked and sunk, and the steamship dock received a direct hit and suffered severe damage.

On October 17, Vidkun Quisling gave the order to evacuate the counties of Finnmark and Troms. Refusal to comply would be punished with fines of up to 100,000 kroner or imprisonment for up to five years. Everyone was required to move south. Minister Lie then issued an announcement to the population, stating that life under Soviet occupation would be intolerable: "Men and women of Norway,

I have personally seen the conditions in Bolshevik Russia and I know what it will mean to a superior people like the Norwegians. It means murder and plunder, terror and arbitrariness, rape, godlessness and moral deterioration."

All buildings were leveled, and all houses burned. Jonas Lie gave a speech on October 21 at the entrance to the mine tunnel in Bjørnevatn, where the inhabitants of Kirkenes had sought shelter from the bombing. He concluded his speech with these words: "Tomorrow is the deadline. Those who refuse to follow orders will be considered our enemies and will be treated accordingly. Tomorrow evening at 7 p.m. the 'Iron Curtain' will fall, and then there will be no recourse."

An endless line of soldiers withdrew that October, eventually totaling more than 200,000 men. Additional troops joined the retreat from defense works, coastal forts, and airstrips. A myriad of vehicles were used, including horse-drawn carts, but many retreated on foot. Endless lines of refugees were herded away from their homes, already reduced to ash across Finnmark, as civilians were forced to evacuate alongside soldiers. They joined columns of ragged, starving prisoners of war, guarded by German soldiers. In Kirkenes, there had been nine prison camps of various kinds, including those for prisoners of war, political prisoners, deserters, criminals, and women with venereal diseases. Most prisoners in the region came from the Soviet Union, many of whom did not survive. They died during the evacuation, and their bodies were discarded at the roadside.

Across Norway, food supplies were more limited than ever. Lack of food and ration cards had been part of daily life throughout the German occupation, but the situation worsened toward the end of the war. Over the following months, repeated notices were sent to fishermen and merchants, encouraging all producers to do their utmost to provide the population with the food it desperately needed. These notices emphasized that a substantial part of the herring and Lofoten cod catch still went to the Germans, who had priority. Wealthy Norwegians were able to obtain fish at high prices, although this was prohibited and punishable by death.

Quite a few fishermen and merchants sold to the Germans at black market prices. A February announcement from the Home Front stated that this was considered treason and would be dealt with accordingly. Sabotage was encouraged by the underground, which demanded that deliveries of fish be as small as possible and that everything possible be done to delay shipments. A shortage of barrels or tainted herring could be blamed.

Hammerfest Must Burn

On October 29, 1944, the first notices announcing the forced evacuation of Hammerfest appeared. Posters were pasted up around town—by the harbor, in public spaces, in shops, and offices. Quisling's ministers, Jonas Lie and Johan Lippestad, arrived from Kirkenes and were seen inspecting the streets of Hammerfest. The town was to be burned systematically, section by section. People who did not follow orders would be rounded up by the Wehrmacht or the Norwegian State Police. A report on the scorched-earth destruction of Hammerfest was submitted to the Nuremberg war crime hearings after the war.

The first area to be burned was Fuglenes, the location of the Lohmann factory and the prison camp, which held many female workers from the East. All buildings were to be completely vacated by noon on Monday, October 30.

17

EVACUATION

On November 1, Anny and her workmates in the Hammerfest factory were ordered to board the fishing vessel *Kveita* (Halibut). She was twenty years old and four months pregnant at the time, having formed an attachment with a young Norwegian factory worker named Jacob Evensen. In fact, by that time, Anny and Jacob had become engaged.

When we interviewed Anny in 2015, she recalled that the Germans managing the factory in Hammerfest had already prepared for evacuation, renting buildings belonging to Nordland Saltlager further south, in Svolvær in the Lofoten Islands. Months earlier, much of the refrigeration equipment had been dismantled and transported there by boat. It is unclear from the records whether it was reinstalled in the factory, although we know from eyewitnesses that Lohmann's factory was operational by early 1945 and that the Soviet women were at work there early that spring.

According to Dr. Gustav Vig, many of the Ukrainian women had diphtheria and were in St. Elisabeth Hospital. Dr. Vig could not recall "whether or not the Germans took care of the imprisoned girls," nor did he "know how they arranged for their transportation south."

The old, red-painted factory buildings in Svolvær, where the Hammerfest operation was moved in late 1944. (Photo: Liv Mjelde.)

However, he did remember that, following the war, when people returned, he "heard that there were four dead in the chapel in Hammerfest, and two of them had been diphtheria patients."

No data exists concerning the identity or fate of the women who perished, and Anny did not know what had happened to them during those chaotic days at the end of the war.

Anny remembers the sea voyage on the *Kveita* and the arrival at Svolvær quite well:

> *"We were like a flock of sheep; we were hurried on board and were not told why or where we were going. But when you are a young, strong girl and together with people you know, you don't get so scared. We were seasick, of course. I was so sick I was allowed to lie down on a bench in the skipper's quarters with a bucket right by me."*

There can be big swells in the Loppa Sea, even in pleasant weather conditions. This stretch of the North Sea is notorious for making most people not accustomed to sailing feel the debilitating effects of seasickness. After weeks of travel on different boats, they reached their destination. None had any inkling that their new home had its own tragic history in the war.

Svolvær's War Years

In Svolvær, the unassuming old post office building is home to a striking collection of World War II artifacts. It is here that William Hakvaag oversees the Lofoten War Remembrance Museum, located close to the pier where the coastal express *Hurtigruten* docks twice daily, as it has done for decades. He meets the coastal steamers twice a day, the northbound and the southbound. Meeting the ships' passengers, mainly tourists from across the globe, he delights in sharing his unique collection and abundant stories about World War II. The museum opened its doors in 1996 and is the result of years of William's unflagging work to conserve memories of the war for the world.

William has led a varied life, training as an engineer and working for years as a foreman in a sanitation company. His mother, Ingeborg Klausen Hakvaag, had been conscripted to work for the German war effort during the occupation. Among other jobs, she worked on the factory ship *D/S Hamburg*, which sank during a British bombing raid on the Lofoten Islands. After this, William's mother was ordered to start work at Frostfilet, where she was employed at the switchboard. She joined a group of Frostfilet workers who smuggled fish to help feed Soviet prisoners hiding in the attic of the hospital in central Bodø at the time. She also witnessed the Allied air attack known as Operation Leader, on October 4, 1943, when fourteen Douglas bombers and six Wildcats attacked the port. Their goal was to sink the German cargo ships transporting frozen fish to the German armies. The eighty-six-meter-long ship *D/S Rabat* sank that day. One torpedo went right underneath the pier where William's mother was working. Although it did not explode, the entire raid significantly slowed production.

On a June day in 2011, William meets us at the museum. In his cluttered office at the back of the building, we gather around a table buried in papers and every imaginable type of book. He serves steaming mugs of coffee, each cup painted with the museum's name. Pushing papers and books to one side, we manage to place our cups on the table. At our first meeting, his facial expression is cautious and somewhat skeptical, but as soon as we begin sharing our story about a coincidental encounter with a child born to

Soviet parents in a prison camp at Langstranda during the final days of World War II, his eyes light up. We have many stories to exchange. He makes it clear that his interest in the war—and in establishing this museum—must always avoid reopening old wounds. Rather than treat any one perspective as definitive, he embraces the messy, contradictory currents of opinion surrounding the years leading up to World War II.

The museum's four rooms are packed floor to ceiling with authentic wartime objects. William discovered most of the artifacts in Norway, but he has also attended auctions in Germany and, in recent years, acquired further treasures via the internet. On display is a collection of objects made by Soviet prisoners, including carved birds, pecking chickens on trays, and decorated boxes fashioned from tin plates. These objects became a kind of currency and were often bartered for food and clothing; many are still found in Norwegian homes. These works of art are a testament to craftsmanship, especially given the circumstances under which they were created.

Also included are photographs of Soviet women celebrating liberation alongside jubilant Norwegians in 1945. The prison uniforms of the Svolvær inmates are on display, as are the traditional garments of a Sámi guide. The Sámi, with their deep knowledge of the northern Norwegian wilderness, helped many flee occupied Norway and cross the border into Sweden. Notably, this museum is the first in Norway to honor the members of the Sámi Nation who assisted so many refugees during the occupation.

Operation Claymore

The Lofoten War Memory Museum has two rooms dedicated to Operation Claymore. While famous as one of the most vital intelligence-gathering operations of the war, it is less well known that one of its objectives was to destroy the German fishing industry and disrupt the production of glycerin—a crucial ingredient in ammunition manufacturing.

In March 1941, the *D/S Hamburg,* a well-equipped and modern factory ship designed for fish processing, lay in the harbor at Svolvær. The ship had been sent to Norway in the spring of 1940 and had previously been stationed at both Hammerfest and Melbu. German prisoners and Wehrmacht soldiers worked on the ship, alongside Norwegians. The Hamburg-based company Andersen & Co owned the ship, which was intended for use along the Norwegian coast, where rich catches could be harvested, processed, and shipped to Germany. It could produce up to forty metric tons of frozen fish fillets per day, in addition to fishmeal and cod-liver oil. Other vessels with freezer capacity transported the fish from Lofoten to Cuxhaven and Altona in Germany.

Early on March 4, 1941, the British bombed the *D/S Hamburg* while it lay berthed at Svinøya Island. The ship sank. Crew members and workers who reacted quickly jumped into the sea and swam across the bay to Svolvær. The water was icy, and many were poor swimmers unable to survive the cold. Others went down with the ship. William Hakvaag's mother, Ingeborg, was aboard the last lifeboat as the ship sank. She remembered passengers hunched down as bullets whistled past their ears. Nobody in that lifeboat died, but one person was shot in the knee. Local residents helped survivors ashore. It was still winter, and large snowdrifts covered the town. The townspeople provided clothing and blankets to keep the survivors alive.

For many years, the wreck of the factory ship remained at the bottom of the sea. Pieces of it can still be seen today. Eyewitness Gunnar Andersen, born in 1940, recalled seeing parts of the ship when he rowed his boat above the wreck as a teenager: "It was a sinister and frightening sight, and I was sure there were many dead Germans down there."

The attackers also bombed the cod-liver oil and herring oil factories at Svinøya, and oil tankers were set on fire. During the action on March 4, British troops managed to disable the German trawler *Krebs* ("Crayfish"). The vessel caught fire, and the crew ran it aground on a reef. As the trawler burned, a British boarding party searched it and confiscated stacks of documents, maps, codebooks, encrypted telegrams, and a set of extra rotors for the Enigma encryption machine. Within days, this intelligence allowed the British to decode encrypted German naval communications sent via Enigma. All materials were analyzed at the British codebreaking center at Bletchley Park, north of London. This discovery aboard the disabled trawler proved vital to the Allies, who were now able to decipher future German war plans.

Members of Operation Claymore went ashore at various locations in Lofoten. According to eyewitness Eva Rosenberg, "They got a lot done in seven hours." More than twenty-two British warships took part in the operation, along with three hundred British sailors and fifty-two Norwegians. One of them was Martin Linge from the Norwegian resistance. He led the first Norwegian resistance unit in Great Britain, Norwegian Independent Company Number 1, which was later renamed Company Linge after his death during the Måløy Raid on the Nazi headquarters in Vågsøy on December 27, 1941.

Allied forces took 212 German prisoners, with Nazis being tracked down with the help of the local population of Svolvær. Twenty-one members of Nasjonal Samling were rounded up and placed on a transport vessel to be taken to the warships anchored outside the shipping lanes.

Many young people seized the opportunity to leave for England with the British ships: 314 left their families and enlisted aboard the naval vessels. Many were sent to training centers in Scotland and Canada and later participated in the fight against the Nazis. Some returned to their occupied homeland as saboteurs.

Troops returning from shore in landing craft after raiding the Lofoten Islands, Norway, March 4, 1941. (Wikimedia Commons)

Chapter 17

A Terrible Aftermath

After the Germans regrouped, a rough period followed for the Lofoten population. Hitler resolved that the attack and the collaboration of the Lofoten people must be avenged. Commissioner Josef Terboven, SS-General Rediess, and Jonas Lie, the Minister of Police, arrived shortly thereafter in Svolvær. One hundred people were arrested, and their homes were burned down. Other homes were destroyed as examples. For instance, the Jansen family home in Svolvær was leveled on March 6, 1941, two days after the Lofoten raid, in retribution for the fact that their son, Jens Jansen, had left for England with the British forces. Houses in the towns of Henningsvær and Stamsund were also razed.

Sixty-four people were imprisoned, first at Hakadal and then at the main detention camp, Grini, both near Oslo. They were the first prisoners to arrive at Grini and were called the "Svolvær hostages."The Wehrmacht also sent reinforcements, including SS soldiers who were remembered for acting very aggressively.

The raid prompted the construction of enormous fortifications in Svolvær. Bunkers, ramparts, and machine-gun emplacements were erected, many on Svinøya. But the work did not stop there. Hitler became obsessively focused on Norway, which he believed would be the "zone of destiny in this war," and he saw the constant air raids and other attacks from Britain as ominous signs. He therefore ordered additional troops and resources to be sent to Norway with the aim of fortifying the entire coastline from Oslofjord in the south to Kirkenes on the Soviet border. Remnants of the massive fortifications can still be seen today, and on Svinøya several installations remain visible. Festung Norwegen ("Fortress Norway"), as the fortification system was known, was built primarily by prisoners of war, at great cost in lives and suffering.

18

FINAL STOP: FROM SVOLVÆR TO LANGSTRANDA

In May 2015 we were back in the north again for more research, hoping to learn more about the women who had been evacuated from Hammerfest in November 1944. William Hakvaag had arranged for us to meet Erling Johan Nilsen, who had worked alongside the Soviet women from Hammerfest at the Lohmann factory during the last year of the war.

Erling was an important eyewitness and was able to contribute new, practical knowledge to this complex story. At the age of nineteen, he had worked with "the Russian girls," as they were called in Svolvær, from the moment they arrived in November 1944 until the end of the war.

We met Erling in the little market square, where he swung elegantly off his bicycle and shook our hands. He was a healthy, vigorous ninety-year-old with clear memories of the war years. Reminding us that the islands were heavily fortified when the Soviet women were brought to Svolvær, Erling led us through the remains of the German defense works and showed us where the prison camp for male prisoners had been, the main fort with its six six-inch cannons, and a large bunker farther up the hill that had likely served as a lookout post.

Erling was born in Svolvær on November 23, 1925. Since 1934, he and his family had lived on Svinøya, one of the islands that make up the town. The family home was near the Artists' House, which for many years has offered shelter to international artists seeking inspiration from the dramatic Lofoten Islands. When my husband and I stayed there during our visit, the artists-in-residence hailed from Sweden, the Netherlands, France, and Japan. One artist from the Netherlands was in the process of creating an underwater sculpture and shared his drawings with us.

A Town Built on Guano and Dried Fish

While the mainland and Svinøya were connected by a bridge in 1963, before that time a small ferry was the only link. Svinøya has long been an important center in the economic development of Svolvær. Dried fish produced there was a major export from the town—a trade controlled by the wealthy Berg family since the early 1800s. The dried fish was sold in markets across Europe and—less celebrated—used as protein to sustain enslaved people working on sugar plantations in the Caribbean. A "fish guano" factory was established on Svinøya in the 1880s, producing highly profitable fish-based fertilizer.

Erling's father worked at the guano factory, but he also sometimes took jobs as a seaman on freighters along the coast. The family was very poor before the war. Erling would gather lumps of guano to sell, eventually saving enough money to buy a suit for his confirmation. He finished school in 1940 and quickly found work at a factory on Bukkedauen, a small island between Storøya and Svinøya, where he made wooden boxes for transporting fish.

At the time, the factory was owned by Gidske Jakobsen, a colorful woman from Narvik who was one of Norway's first female airplane pilots and even owned her own airline. In 1941, the Germans appropriated the factory, but after briefly losing his job, Erling continued to work there making boxes, packing them with fish, and loading them onto vessels bound for Germany. He remembered that his pay came in a yellow envelope marked with the company name Fischeinkauf A/S. The Germans paid well: 2.30 kroner per hour, which was more than

Norwegians had paid. After the war, he continued working in fish production and recalled how salaries dropped back to prewar levels when the Germans left.

War, however, inevitably alters established rules. There was no opportunity to export dried fish during the German occupation, so the Berg family chose to cooperate with the Fischeinkauf company regarding fishing rights and processing. The famous Lofoten cod still had to be processed despite the ongoing conflict. The fishing boats arrived and were unloaded; the fish heads and tongues were cut off, and the liver and roe removed. The fish were cleaned and weighed, then either salted or iced down in boxes. Once filled, the boxes were loaded onto ships and sent to Germany. Although all the fish-freezing machinery from Hammerfest was brought to the Bergs' dock in 1944 and part of it reassembled in the production area, Erling said that frozen fillet production never got off the ground.

This is also what Anny remembered: the fish were not filleted, and the freezing equipment was not used. In other words, fish preparation was done the old-fashioned way.

The "Russian Girls" Arrive

The factory building where Erling and the Soviet women worked together is there to this day, but the barracks they lived in are gone. In springtime, fish are hung from sapling frames several meters high, and their strong odor attracts endless flocks of seabirds. Erling Nilsen is a unique eyewitness to these events, clearly remembering the day the women landed at the quay in Svolvær, from which they were taken in rowboats to Svinøya. A few of the women carried children in their arms, while others, like Anny, were pregnant (see previous chapter).

Our best estimate is that 182 women and four children arrived in Svolvær in November 1944. When they left Hammerfest, they numbered 300. Sixty were sent to Frostfilet in Bodø, and sixty to the plant in Trondheim.

During the cod high season, they worked together from seven in the morning until five in the afternoon. At first, they were housed in barracks not far from Erling's family home. He saw the "Russian girls" pass by as they moved to and from work, and he recalled that they would be singing despite the guards surrounding them. They sang as they marched, while they worked, and in the evenings.

Erling described the women as kind and pleasant to work with, but certainly knowing their own minds and possessing immense integrity. Although they did not share a common language with the local people, they managed to communicate through gestures and laughter. He also remembered the letter "O" sewn onto the upper part of their jacket sleeves.

They formed a choir, and when they rehearsed, Norwegians would gather outside the barracks to listen during that long, dark winter of 1944–45. When the beautiful, melancholy songs resounded in the night, combined with a starry sky and the northern lights, it was an experience no one would forget. Erling says it has remained with him for the rest of his life.

The women in the Svolvær prison camp enjoyed considerable freedom during the final months of the war. Erling remembers that they were permitted to go to the mainland. They were allowed to go to the cinema, as they had been in Hammerfest, enjoying movies such as the *Deutsche Wochenschau* (The German Weekly Show), a newsreel series that was an integral part of German propaganda. Also, starting on January 1, 1945, they obtained the same status as other foreign workers in the service of the Germans. Nilsen recalls that they were able to circulate outside the camp and did not have any serious problems with the guards. In 1945, the Nazis could see defeat coming; this influenced the guards who were responsible for the health and welfare of the prisoners who feared reprisals. They no longer acted as the brutal victors of 1940. Prisoners in many labor camps were thus given increased liberties during this last phase of the war.

In this new atmosphere, the camp commandant at Svolvær was amenable to requests from prisoners. One such request came from Anny, who asked to be transferred to the Frostfilet factory at Langstranda in Bodø after learning that her fiancé, Jacob Evensen, was working there. The commandant granted the heavily pregnant Anny permission to transfer to Langstranda. On March 11, 1945, her son Jonni was born.

Return to Langstranda

As in Svolvær, the situation had improved in Langstranda. This was confirmed by Torbjørn Feiring, whom we interviewed in Bodø in May 2015. At ninety years old, he was vibrant, possessed a sharp memory, and offered thoughtful reflections on his work during the war. He was fifteen when the war began and spent much of the war years working as a fisherman's helper on various boats and at the Schjølberg factory during the Lofoten cod high season. He recalled sailing to Langstranda, where they sold fish to the Fischeinkauf purchasing organization. He spoke disapprovingly of the many boat owners who grew wealthy working for the Germans, but also noted that many fishing boats were confiscated.

Torbjørn also witnessed the arrival of Soviet prisoners in May 1942. He vividly remembered them singing as they marched from the quay through the city, and later enjoying the sound of a Russian choir at Frostfilet.

In the spring of 1945, Torbjørn worked in the packing house at the Norwegian-owned Schjølberg fish factory and lived in the apartment building owned by the company. This was located across from two frozen fish factories, the other being the German Frostfilet. He recalled that the Schjølberg owner supervised production daily and that only men worked in the factory—no Germans were present during his time there.

He frequently encountered the forced laborers over the years. The two plants were connected by a bridge, and the prisoners made a hole in the wall on the German side through which informal trading took place. Torbjørn remembered passing balls of wool yarn from his mother through the hole, in exchange for black pepper. He also recalled that "Ukrainians," as they were called in Bodø, sometimes visited the apartment where he lived with other Norwegian workers in the evenings. Both sides understood a little German, but they lacked a shared language. They communicated with gestures and exchanged handicrafts and tobacco.

Like Erling Nilsen, Torbjørn remembered changes in the treatment of laborers at the fish factories and barracks over the course of the war.

In Langstranda, this included access to medical care, a field hospital, and showers at the plant.

Toward the end of the war, further directives from Berlin and Oslo ordered that the prisoners be paid for their work. With characteristic bureaucratic precision, the Germans registered the prisoners as workers. Each prisoner had a work card on which their output was recorded. Different kinds of work were paid at different rates, although Norwegians always earned more than forced laborers, and men more than women. The prisoners received tobacco, though only half as much as German soldiers. The Soviets were given Machorka, a low-quality brand. Housing, food, and clothing were all deducted from their pay. In total, forced laborers received an average of seventy-three kroner per month in 1945.

PART V

LIBERATION AND REPATRIATION

19

THE REICH COLLAPSES

The chaos at the end of the war took different forms in different countries. Italy's Benito Mussolini, *Il Duce,* and his lover Clara Petacci were shot and then hanged from a scaffold by a furious mob in Milan on April 28, 1945. On the Eastern front, 1.5 million Red Army soldiers had fought their way to victory in Berlin, where Adolf Hitler and Eva Braun committed suicide on April 30. An unconditional surrender agreement was signed in Reims on May 7 by General Jodl, the new German Chief of Staff.

In Norway, the Nasjonal Samling government carried on into the early days of May. As late as May 7, 1945, Vidkun Quisling proclaimed on the front page of the newspaper *Aftenposten* that his was Norway's legitimate and proper government. An order on the front page declared that "blackout curtains must be in place between 9:57 p.m. and 4:38 a.m.," as a rain of bombs was expected across the country. Another article reported the ceasefire declared in Denmark, northwest Germany, the Netherlands, and Italy, but repeated Berlin's latest proclamation in a subheading: "All German military forces that are not touched by the ceasefire are continuing the struggle against the Soviet-Russians." Nonetheless, everyday life continued. On the same day, the newspaper noted that 240 children had been confirmed in churches on

Sunday, May 6, and ten children had been born in Oslo and its environs.

Unlike socialist and liberal newspapers, which were closed during the occupation, *Aftenposten* had been published throughout the war, serving as a propaganda vehicle for the Quisling government and Berlin. The country's leading conservative newspaper, it had supported Hitler's Germany as far back as the early 1930s. In 1935, for instance, the editors attacked the Norwegian Nobel Committee for awarding that year's Peace Prize to the editor and peace advocate Carl von Ossietzky. That same year, the newspaper received a note of congratulations from Hitler's propaganda minister, Joseph Goebbels, on its seventy-fifth anniversary. The May 7 edition of *Aftenposten* led with an article on Hitler's death by the Norwegian novelist and Nobel Laureate Knut Hamsun, who lauded Hitler as "a warrior, a warrior for humankind, and a prophet of the gospel of justice for all nations."

May 8, 1945, Liberation Day. "The newspaper Oslo-Pressen is eagerly read, with the Norwegian flag on the building behind." (Photo: Håkon Præstkvern, Hedmark Museum.)

Unsurprisingly, the paper was shut down after that edition—but only for a week, reappearing on May 14. Like other conservative newspapers, *Aftenposten*'s only punishment aside from the brief closure was a small fine.

On May 8, the first edition of a new paper, *Oslo-Pressen*, appeared on the streets of the capital, having been produced in secret on the premises of *Aftenposten*. For several days, it was the only newspaper published in the country. In it, the leadership of the Home Front announced that "our struggle has been crowned by victory. Norway is free once again." It went on to state: "Our souls are filled with joy, our hearts with gratitude toward those who fell in the battle and toward all those who contributed to the fight toward victory. The enemy has now capitulated and soon we will be the rulers of our land. But remember —capitulation is not the same as peace. The enemy still has weapons."

The momentum of liberation was unstoppable, and one gratifying event swiftly followed another. Early Thursday morning, May 10, Major General Roy Urquhart arrived on Norwegian soil as one of the first members of Britain's military forces.

Norwegian police troops arrived from Sweden, along with English and Norwegian paratroopers. On May 13, Crown Prince Olav and a group of cabinet ministers arrived from London.

And yet, the situation was far from clear—both internationally and within Norway. General Jodl's signature affirming unconditional surrender on both the Eastern and Western Fronts was regarded by the Soviet Union as a surprise move by the Western Allies in a game of chess. Stalin considered the modest ceremony that had taken place at General Eisenhower's headquarters in a schoolhouse in Reims unworthy of the scale and suffering of the war Europe had endured. General Smith of the United States had alone accepted the surrender on behalf of the Allies, with General Susloparov of the Soviet Union and General Sevez of France acting only as witnesses. It was unthinkable that the Soviet Union would be represented merely by an observer —and in any case, the Wehrmacht was still resisting in several locations on May 7 and 8. The war was not yet over. The weapons had not been laid down, and contradictions and political controversy persisted. In the end, the Allies agreed that the ceremony at Reims would be regarded as provisional, and the final capitulation accords were signed in Berlin at 12:43 a.m. on May 9, 1945.

There was also great uncertainty about the situation in Norway. Quisling and members of Nasjonal Samling had not surrendered. Reichskommissar Josef Terboven gathered twenty-five leading officers prepared to fight for their survival at the famous Grand Hotel in central Oslo—on the same evening that Marshal Georgy Zhukov's troops advanced toward the Seelow Heights and Reichstrasse 1 in Berlin. At that point, around 350,000 German soldiers remained in Norway. Would the Wehrmacht surrender, or would they take up arms?

And how would the resistance movement respond? In France, liberated in August 1944, the resistance took the law into its own hands across the country, and between 40,000 and 50,000 collaborators were killed in an avalanche of retribution. Rage and a thirst for revenge after five years of German occupation were also present in Norway. An estimated 45,000 Norwegian resistance fighters and political activists had been arrested during the occupation, of whom 1,400 perished. Was a peaceful transition from occupation to independence possible?

To understand what actually happened in Norway—and how it affected the women and men who are the subjects of this book—we must first examine the efforts made to prepare for a peaceful transition from Nazi terror to freedom. Most of the strategic planning took place in London, where the government-in-exile had been established. Another part lay in the hands of the underground leaders of the Home Front and its armed wing, MILORG (short for Militær Organisasjon). Sweden became an important partner in the later years of the war. Beginning in 1943, approximately 14,700 Norwegians were trained in Sweden to take part in the liberation of Norway. They were to move in once the Germans capitulated, ensuring that the country was prepared for any eventuality and able to assert itself in international negotiations. As we will see in the following chapter, local plans were also made across the country, and Home Front units stood ready for action.

20

LANGSTRANDA LIBERATED

We met Arne Nystad in Bodø in May 2015. He was another vibrant ninety-year-old with an excellent memory and strong political views.

Arne was approaching his twentieth birthday in the spring of 1945, and was in his final year of school in Bodø. He and his father had followed the events on the Eastern front on the map, feeling great sympathy for the Soviet effort. But there had also been Nazi supporters in his class, and for several years the atmosphere in the classroom had been heavy with unspoken political tensions. The young Nazi sympathizers had repeatedly demonstrated arrogance and self-satisfaction during the occupation. However, the situation had now changed. After the defeat at Stalingrad, many Nazi supporters began to change their tune. They were no longer convinced of their own superiority or of the inevitability of victory for the Third Reich.

Arne's teacher, Professor Moseide, invited two or three students—including Arne—to join the Home Front. Moseide was part of a resistance cell in Bodø and had connections throughout the region. On May 7, Arne joined a group of around ten young men in Bodø for their first meeting. They were issued rifles and told their mission was to liberate the prison camp at Langstranda.

The head of the Home Front in Nordland County was Dr. Anton Johnson—the doctor who had worked for years at the hospital in Bodø (see chapter 9). An idealist with strong leadership qualities and a pleasant nature, Dr. Johnson's mettle was put to the test in those tense days. He played an extraordinary role during the liberation period, not only at Langstranda but across Nordland more broadly.

As the collapse of German control drew near, Dr. Johnson had established a special committee within the local Home Front to maintain contact with the prison camps in Nordland. The committee members included a local agriculture ministry official named Hovde, Frostfilet owner Ragnar Schjølberg, Dr. Friis, Secretary Otto Hansen, and Gunnar Moe. In May 1945, they sent a report to Home Front headquarters stating that three members of management and five workers at Frostfilet had been recruited to the resistance. Among these workers was Jacob Evensen, whose fiancée, Anny Koljada, was then in the women's barracks at the prison camp with their son, Jonni.

The physical takeover of the prison camp at Langstranda occurred on May 8, but the situation was initially quite confused. Already on May 7, an announcement had been issued by the temporary Norwegian administration in Nordland to all prisoners of war, declaring that they were now free. The German and Norwegian guards could no longer threaten them with weapons or punishment, and the gates would be opened. Repatriation would be organized, but it had to happen in an orderly fashion. The announcement warned that if prisoners attempted to leave on their own, the result would be confusion and chaos. It further stated that the necessary orders and directives would soon be communicated by the Allied High Command or the Norwegian government.

Rumors were circulating in every direction, and it was vital to maintain order—precisely the task that Arne Nystad's group had been assigned. The leader of Arne's team was a sergeant from the Norwegian police troops who had recently returned from Sweden.

Seventy years later, he vividly recalled that when his team arrived, German guards armed with machine guns stood in front of every barrack at the Langstranda prison camp. As his team approached the gate, they were met by cries of "*Vansinn, Vansinn, Untermenschen*" ("Insane, insane, sub-humans") from the German commandant. To the Germans, the prisoners—Slavs—were not worthy of liberation. The commandant also shouted that the prisoners were armed and planning to take the town by storm and establish a Soviet state.

It is possible that the commandant was unaware of the formal German capitulation in Norway, which had been announced by the German High Command in Lillehammer on May 7 around 9 p.m., to take effect at 10 a.m. on May 8. Whether or not the memorandum had reached him, the Germans did not surrender that morning. The Norwegian sergeant had to call for reinforcements, and soon a bus arrived with more armed Norwegians and representatives of the Norwegian authorities.

Fortunately, Dr. Johnson was among them, and when the prisoners saw him, they began to shout in welcome. The doctor was well known to them, having treated several at the Bodø Hospital. Dr. Johnson was able to negotiate a peaceful takeover, making it clear that the inmates—of all nationalities—were no longer prisoners but free men, women, and children.

Despite this initial success, it did not take long for internal camp conflicts to erupt. Among the 952 women and men of various nationalities at Langstranda that morning, national and political divisions and personal vendettas surfaced. Some prisoners had worked closely with the Nazis as capos and now had to be protected from the rage of fellow inmates. There is evidence that Ukrainian, Latvian, Estonian, Belarusian, and Volga-German prisoners were the most likely to be accused of collaboration as so-called "capos," or assistants to the guards, both in the factory and the camp. Some may have been "Vlasov sympathizers," named after Russian commander General Andrei Vlasov, who had played an important role in the Battle of Moscow and had once been one of Stalin's favored generals (see chapter 8).

Sent to lead a breakout attempt during the siege of Leningrad, Vlasov and his men were surrounded and taken prisoner. He defected to the German side and became a figurehead for a propaganda effort designed to persuade Soviet prisoners across Europe to reject communism and fight under his anti-Soviet command. Hundreds of Soviet prisoners in Norway were recruited—many of whom had served as camp police or had been made capos. Vlasov himself was eventually returned to the USSR, tortured, and executed shortly after the war ended.

Arne Nystad recalled how six or seven prisoners—two of them women—had to be locked in a spare room at Langstranda until Dr. Johnson could arrange their transfer to the Bodø penitentiary.

Dr. Johnson's name comes up repeatedly in accounts of this period. For example, a report by Dr. Leiv Kreyberg—a figure whom we will meet later—tells of an episode in which Johnson's intervention avoided what might have become a dangerous situation:

> *At Frostfilet A/S, the Russian forced laborers had, during their imprisonment, fed some pigs with waste products from the factory. They therefore felt attached to these pigs with strong emotional bonds, and one afternoon they decided they wanted to butcher the pigs and make a celebratory meal to commemorate their fallen brothers. When rumors of this intent were heard in Bodø, an action was initiated by the agricultural authorities to save the pigs in order to support Norwegian pig breeding. When the vehicle arrived to fetch the pigs, the mood became somewhat heated and a riot was brewing. A delegation was organized to demand military intervention to protect Norwegian agricultural interests. The case was fortunately placed in the hands of the Home Front's chief physician, Dr. Johnson, who went down to Frostfilet A/S and familiarized himself with the situation. Dr. Johnson found that the Russians' feelings were easily understood. In addition, it appeared that most of the pigs had been castrated and were therefore not of particular interest for Norwegian pig breeding. However, there was one pregnant sow, well suited to the purpose. Dr. Johnson therefore judged—in a decision worthy of Solomon—that the sow would go to Norwegian agriculture and the castrated pigs would be awarded to the Russians for their celebratory meal.*

Negotiations to Send the Prisoners Home

At the Moscow Conference in September 1944, an agreement had been reached between the British Foreign Secretary, Anthony Eden, and the Soviet Commissar of Foreign Affairs, Vyacheslav Mikhailovich Molotov, confirming that all Soviet citizens would be sent back to the Soviet

Union, and British citizens would be returned to England from areas controlled by the Soviet Union. In the case of Soviet army prisoners, a major concern was Order No. 227, issued in July 1942, under which soldiers deemed to be cowards or to have caused panic could be executed on the spot or sent to special penal battalions to be used as cannon fodder. Was this message still imprinted on the minds of freed prisoners? Or had they heard about Stalin's amnesty declaration, promising that when they returned home, they would be pardoned?

This amnesty also freed more than a million people from the labor camps in Siberia. Paradoxically, petty criminals who had been sent to labor camps benefited from the amnesty, while political prisoners had their sentences extended. Eight years were added to Alexander Solzhenitsyn's sentence, which he described as "Stalin's cruel joke on the political prisoners." Prisoners of war were registered and investigated but would not be punished.

Some of the primarily youthful inmates at Langstranda had other questions on their minds. Young women and men had formed attachments and had children together. Would they be able to continue seeing each other and raise their children together?

None of them knew what awaited them on their return. What had happened to parents, siblings, and friends? Did they have a home to come back to? For several years, they had been bombarded with propaganda about the Nazis' victories in the Soviet Union, including the battles of Kursk and Moscow and the sieges of Leningrad and Stalingrad. But rumors had also reached Langstranda about the Allies' advance, the Leningrad population's fight to survive, and the fierce battles at Kursk and Stalingrad. Who had survived? Who would still be alive and expecting them? What was the current political situation in general, and particularly in the Soviet Union?

Galina and Fedor, along with the 100,000 other Soviet prisoners in 500 prison camps all over Norway, did not know what the future would bring. But one thing was certain: their time and hardship at Frostfilet were over. The prison camps were opened. They were no longer prisoners. They were free and included among the victorious Allies.

A sense of liberation can be seen in one of the photos that Yuri found in his mother's partially dated "Bodø" wallet (see chapter 2). Unlike other photos in the wallet, in which Galina and Fedor appear to be standing on snow, the group photo seems to have been taken in bright sunlight, with half of the group sitting on grass. Most of the group are women, and two hold infants in their arms. The photo is lent a festive air by the smiles on many of the women's faces and the appearance of a young man in the front row playing an accordion. Galina stands on the far right with her hand on the shoulder of the woman next to her.

On the far left, we see another person from our narrative: Arkady Mozerin, the partner of Marfa Stepina (see chapter 16). His cap and vest are the same as in an earlier photo taken with Marfa, and his wary expression hasn't changed—in contrast to the happiness on many of the women's faces.

Spring 1945, outside a prison camp barracks, Arkady Mozerin stands far left, while Galina Korolenko can be seen far right. (Photo: Yuri Salnikov.)

Celebration...and Looting

The evacuation of Frostfilet and Langstranda proceeded quickly and calmly, thanks to the effort of Dr. Johnson. A total of 792 men, 160 women, and fifty-two children were finally released. The Germans left Langstranda at 1:30 p.m. on May 11. The detested barbed-wire gates were opened. The guards and Hird members were arrested and taken away. The prisoners were suddenly the victors. They could move about freely outside the camp. They could go into the adjoining town of Bodø. They could meet their Norwegian allies. As a general policy, the Norwegian authorities encouraged the liberated Soviet prisoners across the country to form their local soviets (local councils), choose leaders, establish a local military police to keep order, and write the history of their camp.

There were great celebrations in Bodø, in which the prisoners at Langstranda were invited to take part. But not everyone could participate—there were simply too many. Instead, the elected leaders selected several hundred who marched into the center of town singing Russian songs. Norwegians under the leadership of Bernt Balchen from the Royal Norbotten Air Base also arrived. Many of them had been in Luleå, waiting for the liberation of Norway. Norwegian police troops from Sweden, Englishmen from the Special Operations Executive (SOE), and Americans from the United States' Office of Strategic Services (OSS) were given a warm welcome by Norwegians and Soviets in the streets of Bodø, as they were all over Norway.

On May 17, the first planeloads of Americans and food supplies arrived. Once again there were celebrations, as the Soviet citizens marched with the Norwegians celebrating Norway's Constitution Day. They carried portraits of Josef Stalin. On this particular Constitution Day, Bodø—and all of Norway—were intoxicated with joy; they had not been allowed to celebrate this day for five long years.

But Bodø and Nordland were facing great challenges. Nordland County extends for 500 kilometers and has always been sparsely populated. At the end of the war, roads and telecommunications were in poor condition. The county also housed the largest concentration of prison camps in Norway. Dr. Johnson described the situation as follows:

> *"With capitulation we found ourselves on May 8 faced with a big task. Almost 30,000 starving, terrorized prisoners, filled with hatred for the Germans; more*

> *than a third, or 130,000 German soldiers, of the country's combined occupying forces; and thousands of deported foreigners, were being kept in our sparsely populated rural county where the Norwegian population was practically drowning in the swarm of foreigners. In addition, we had the Gestapo as well as a lot of armed, desperate Norwegian Nazis with the Hird and Nazi police."*

Inevitably, there was disorder amid the general calm. The block-houses were looted. The owner of the Norwegian-run Frostfilet factory, Ragnar Schjølberg, recalled in his notes of June 6 and 8 that as soon as the Germans left at 1:30 p.m. on May 11, the Soviets began looting the houses where the Germans had lived. Help from the Home Front was requested but proved inadequate. He continued:

> *"The factory has been broken into every time the Russians used the wash-rooms... Yesterday afternoon Frostfilet's transformer room, the electrical supply warehouse, and office were broken into."*

Soviet guards were responsible for guarding the factory. Once again, Schjølberg criticized the Soviets' behavior, as he had done during the occupation.

A different kind of looting also took place at Frostfilet. The Allies believed that the Wehrmacht's advances on land, at sea, and in the air were largely due to the technological superiority developed in Germany since the time of Chancellor Otto von Bismarck. Ian Fleming, later the famed author of the James Bond books, was then an aide-de-camp to the head of intelligence in the British Royal Navy. Fleming led the top-secret naval unit known as the Thirty Assault Unit. The unit had one main purpose: to seize military and industrial documents and matériel from the enemy and send them to England. The Thirty Assault Unit was to move in ahead of the army, before the enemy had time to destroy them. Laboratories and factories were exhaustively searched, including Frostfilet at Langstranda, which was considered to be Europe's most advanced fish processing plant, with its cutting-edge filleting machinery and refrigeration technology. The Royal Navy arrived and confiscated all of it—lock, stock, and barrel.

21

"UNTIL WE MEET AGAIN"

By many measures, the prisoners at Frostfilet had been fortunate. In the photographs, none of them looks starved. Their access to food improved as the war went on, and they appeared to be in good health. They were not subjected to the Nazis' Hunger Plan targeting "sub-human" races, as the Soviets in other camps in Nordland were. Compared with other prisoners, they had decent accommodations. They had showers at the factory, a field hospital nearby, and illness and death did not constantly stalk them. Nor were their workloads as severe as those of other prisoners in the region. In contrast, the prisoners working in road and railroad construction suffered entirely different conditions and work situations. Miserable sanitation, lack of clothing, illness, and death were part of daily life in the prison camps that lined the Saltfjellet mountain range. The men had built roads across rough mountain passes and constructed the Nordland railroad under the most inhumane conditions.

Much of this was documented by Dr. Leiv Kreyberg, who headed the evacuation of prisoners in Nordland County—an important figure whose reports and the Nordland Archives have been key sources in this work.

Soviet prisoners of war behind barbed wire at Falstad Camp, May 8, 1945. (Photographer Unknown / The Falstad Centre)

Kreyberg returned to Norway on the morning of May 10 after five years in exile. After meeting Brigadier Otto Munthe-Kaas, the zone commander for northern Norway in Narvik, Dr. Kreyberg arrived in Bodø to begin his assignment. He was well qualified for the task. A pathologist by training, he had spent much of the war in Scotland. He had also gained significant experience on the Continent during the liberation of 1944 and had studied practical aspects of mass transportation, interrogation, and delousing.

In a report written in 1946, Dr. Kreyberg detailed the tasks he faced regarding the roughly 26,000 Russians, 1,200 Poles, and 800 Yugoslavs whose repatriation from Nordland County he had to arrange. As far as possible, he wanted the camps organized along national lines and for them to enjoy a degree of self-rule, including the election of their own leaders. The hope was to minimize the need for Norwegian military personnel to be posted as guards. Dr. Kreyberg's responsibilities also included prisoner healthcare, which proved to be especially demanding.

On May 17, he dispatched crews to carry out these assignments in the various districts. The Norwegian forces were to function as a kind of liaison between the Soviets and Germans. Dr. Kreyberg wrote in his directive of May 17:

> The Germans must be treated in a very cool fashion. No tendency toward friendliness is permitted, nor is any impoliteness. The Russians must be treated cordially, possibly with a kind heart. But they must not be encouraged in their bitterness toward the Germans. This Norwegian duty will best succeed with calm and thoughtfulness during this period of disbandment.

Arne Nystad was sent from Bodø to help with the opening of the camps in Saltdal, about 100 kilometers to the southeast. Conditions there were horrific. The approximately 6,000 prisoners of war included a great number of sick men suffering through the spring thaw in wretched barracks constructed high in the mountains. Arne remembered specifically two Russians he met there, Alex and Victor, describing them as "two of life's fun-loving boys." The pair came from the same village in the Crimea, Kratnaodoyiska. Alex had worked for a fishmonger, while Victor had moved to Moscow, where he worked in radio. They had not seen each other for years when they met again at the prison camp in Saltdalen. When Arne met them, they were "riddled with tuberculosis," and he did not know if they would survive. To this day, their memory stays with him.

It is hard to determine the exact final total of the prisoners who died in this part of Nordland. In 1946, Dr. Kreyberg wrote:

> The numbers of prisoners presented must necessarily be approximate because, in part, the Germans did not have a clear idea of the numbers, so on that front, we were given no real information, and in part, the numbers changed by the hour because prisoners died from disease and other more or less normal causes every single day.

Texts on the walls at the Red Cross Narvik Center War Museum state that between 1941 and 1945, there were 27,000 Soviet prisoners in the camps from Rana to Ofoten. Of these, 10,500 died. Of the 2,600 Yugoslavs, some 2,300 perished. However, these figures are probably inaccurate, and we may never know the exact numbers. The Soviet military took the prisoners' index cards back to the Soviet Union in 1945. When the Falstad Research Center was established in 2010, it was impossible to retrieve this material, as the Russian authorities did not want to make the archives available.

We do know, from numbers registered in Luleå, that 24,339 Soviet prisoners of war traveled from Narvik between June and July of 1945. However, Dr. Kreyberg's organization was not alone in preparing the departures. He writes: "The ex-prisoners themselves kept their counts and prepared themselves. The Allies, for their part, organized railroad and steamship transport, so in terms of transportation, it was just the movements from the camps to the loading zones that fell to us."

We also know that bonds of friendship and affection were formed between Russians and Norwegians. Arne Nystad remembers befriending a former prisoner and giving him some of his clothes. They were both interested in radios and promised to stay in touch, but the international political situation made maintaining contact almost impossible. Love was also in the air during this time of euphoria, with real-life consequences. Norwegian women gave birth to children with Soviet fathers in the following year; unfortunately, many of these children are still searching for their fathers. In recent years, the Norwegian Broadcasting Corporation (NRK) successfully traced some of these "lost fathers" in Russia and aired the emotional reunions on television.

Departure

Norwegian police troops, diplomats, and international administration personnel were all installed at Hotel Royal in Narvik in the summer of 1945. Today, the few archives kept at the Narvik Center shed light on the complexities involved in returning tens of thousands of prisoners from Northern Norway to the Soviet Union. Narvik was the point of departure for the Ofoten railroad to the Swedish port of Luleå. There, the Soviet citizens would embark for Finland, where they would find transport for the final leg of their journey home.

The Soviet prisoners had reached Narvik from myriad locations. A report from June 19 notes the expected arrival of the *Freia* with 800

"Russians" from the Drag district, about 100 kilometers southwest of Narvik, leaving only "women and the infirm" still to be collected. On the following day, the *Vøringen* was recorded as coming from Lofoten with 350 people, then returning to collect 170 women, concluding: "Then Lofoten will have been emptied."

This may have included the women from the Lohmann factory in Svolvær. According to a letter dated April 9, 1945, from the Lohmann management to the Reichskommissariat in Oslo, 178 women and four children were set free.

There were two daily trains to Luleå in the period between June 13 and July 11, with the last trainload of Soviet prisoners departing for Luleå in mid-July. A report from June 24 recorded: "Today we are sending off train number 11 and have reached 8,800. With every train, fifty women and 750 men now leave until there are no more women left."

In the end, a total of 24,494 prisoners of war were sent home along this route. Of these, 424 were women and 64 were children. On a system where the total daily capacity was around 1,000 passengers, this was the largest collective transportation in the Ofoten railroad's history. However, this "record" was later surpassed when 30,000 Germans were sent home the same way. The shipments of Germans began on August 3, 1945, and the last trainload left Narvik on September 5, 1945.

A permanent shroud appears to have been lowered over the events of the summer of 1945, when liberated Soviet prisoners were brought by train to Luleå, Sweden. For example, limited evidence of the event appears in newspaper clippings displayed on the walls of the Red Cross Museum in Narvik. Evidently, these train transports were of interest to the contemporary press in both Norway and Sweden. On June 14, 1945, the Narvik newspaper *Ofotens Tidende* carried an announcement from the Allied Information Service in Stockholm stating that arrangements had been made for Soviet citizens to be transported from Norway to Sweden. The announcement goes on to say: "The sixty Swedish journalists who had been permitted to travel to the border to join the first Russian train were later told that this transport must not be reported. Announcement made by NTB (Norwegian Telegraph Office) from Stockholm." The journalists in Sweden received this message on June 13, 1945. It is not clear who decided that these homebound journeys were not to be reported. It is also remarkable that the Ofoten railroad records covering the period from 1944 to 1948 have been destroyed.

Back in Bodø, the prisoners' departure was noted in one of Dr. Kreyberg's reports. Its pages include photos of newly freed eastern prisoners marching down the main street past the Grand Hotel, carrying banners and portraits. Bodø's population lined the streets to say goodbye.

Arne Nystad remembers the departure of the prisoners from Bodø as clearly as their arrival three years earlier. Many left Bodø aboard the *M/S Mungo* from Løvøy pier on July 2, 1945—the same pier where the daily coastal ferry service *Hurtigruten* docks today. Arne stood next to the town's chief of police that day. Knut Støre, who would later save the Frostfilet archives, was also present. Arne recalls everyone on the pier shouting "Do Svidanja" (Russian for "Until we meet again").

Unfortunately, no list exists of those on board the *M/S Mungo* from Bodø to Narvik. But we do know that Galina, Fedor, and Yuri were among those transported to Narvik, continued on to Luleå, and finally made it home to Russia.

22

VALENTINA: A CHILDHOOD UNDER A CLOUD

We have already recounted the stories of Yuri Salnikov and his parents Galina and Fedor, and the difficulties they faced for decades after their return to Russia, not least the mystery that dogged Yuri about the facts of his birth.

Valentina Stepina, the daughter of Marfa Stepina whom we met in chapter 11, faced some of the same problems as Yuri, but with a crucial difference: she had always known that she had been born in Norway. Marfa never hid the story from her. She also knew that her father, Arkady Mozyerin, had been one of the NKVD officers who worked as a slave laborer at Langstranda.

The records show that fifty-one children from Langstranda—thirty-one boys and twenty girls—arrived in Luleå with their mothers. Only two mothers in this group were originally from Russia's major cities: Galina from Leningrad (though she had been abducted farther south in Gzhatsk) and Polina Masajova from Moscow.

Valentina was one of the larger cohort of children whose mothers were abducted from Russia's western oblasts and Ukraine's eastern region. After the devastating battles and scorched-earth campaigns that marked the German invasion and the Great Patriotic War, there was little left to return to after spending time in an internment camp in Vyborg, west of Leningrad.

The camp was where returning prisoners discovered their fate. In general, the women with children were sent back to the same place where they had been captured years earlier. We know a little about these women. Of the four from Kursk, Nadia Valyakova was the only one who brought a child with her into the ruins of her city. Of the twenty young girls from Smolensk, five were pregnant when they returned. Two of the mothers with children were from the Ukrainian cities of Voroshilovgrad (now called Luhansk), and two from Dnipropetrovsk (now Dnipro).

As for Marfa, upon her return to Russia with Valentina, she found her father and one of her sisters in a village near Bryansk where they had built a small house. But her homecoming was not a joyful one. She had no money, and her family had nothing to offer. It was hard to return to her father with a child in her arms and no husband. Officialdom was no help. Marfa wanted to leave Bryansk to find Valentina's father, Arkady, but when she applied for a travel pass, it was denied. When she looked for work, she was limited by an attestation document she received that gave her three months to find employment. The document served as a kind of residency permit but did not allow her to take a permanent job. Instead, she took temporary jobs, often hard forestry work.

In addition to these material hardships, Valentina grew up as the object of insults and harassment, as was her mother. They were called "Norwegian" or "German" and other derogatory terms common in Bryansk. Valentina even remembers neighbors calling them "Norwegian whores," echoing the treatment of the *Lebensborn* children and their mothers described in chapter 7.

Valentina's neighborhood friend, Nadezda Lukatina, was also born at Langstranda, on October 8, 1944. She experienced the same kind of name-calling. The two of them have supported and helped one another throughout their difficult lives to this day.

Valentina never met her father, Arkady. He wrote them a few letters for about a year after their return home, which Valentina believes came from Russia's Far East. He also sent a photo with an inscription on the back: "*To Marfa and Valya in memory of life. Do not forget me when I am no more.*"

Marfa and Valentina's situation looked more hopeful in the 1970s when the Soviet Union accepted reparation funds from the Federal Republic of Germany. The arrangement permitted forced laborers to apply for compensation. However, this required Valentina—now an adult—to convince a Soviet court not only that her mother had been a civilian forced laborer in Norway, but also that Valentina had been born there. In Bodø, Marfa had registered her daughter as Tatyana, naming her after an aunt, but changed the name to Valentina when they returned to Bryansk in 1945. Marfa believed the name Valentina would bring her daughter better luck. However, the name change became a problem when they applied for compensation, as it made the judge suspicious. Fortunately, Valentina ultimately succeeded in having Bodø accepted as her birthplace. As a result, she receives a small pension funded by her former captors.

PART VI

THE RETURN, 2015

23

A GATHERING IN LULEÅ

On Friday, May 8, 2015, under a pale Norrbotten sun, an international gathering unveiled a memorial monument of polished granite in the village of Karlsvik near Luleå in northern Sweden. The monument was a simple, smooth stone made by local stone cutters. Inscribed are the words: "In memory of the 24,339 Soviet soldiers and civilians who were here in 1945 after being liberated from German imprisonment in Norway." The words are accompanied by the image of a dove over barbed wire and a red star. The stone is a memorial to the Soviet prisoners of war and forced laborers from the East who were assembled here, arriving from Narvik by train in the summer of 1945.

It was the first of two days of celebration in Luleå, including exhibits, lectures, and a performance of *Vi minns förr fred* (*We Gather to Commemorate Peace*) in the city hall. It was the seventieth anniversary of the end of World War II, celebrated in many parts of the world in 2015. The festivities were organized by the Russian–Swedish association Sputnik, headquartered in Luleå. Many Russians live and work in Sweden. The founder of the organization, Katerina Ekstrøm, is a St. Petersburg native who relocated after marrying her Swedish husband,

Anders Ekstrøm. The association initiated the construction of this memorial in 2013, and two years later, it was finally in place.

Inauguration of the memorial to Soviet soldiers and prisoners in Karlsvik. From left to right: Elena and Mikhail Salnikov, Valentina Stepina, Yuri Salnikov, his granddaughter Lisa Salnikov, Liv Mjelde, and Richard Daly. (Photo: Lars Gyllenhaal.)

The war's end is celebrated in Luleå on both May 8 and May 9. Although Sweden, along with the Western Allies, commemorates May 8, it is important to the Russian community to mark May 9, as is done in Russia and some former Soviet states. In her speech, Katerina emphasized that the Russian people never want war and that the memorial should be seen as part of an effort to build bridges toward common peaceful goals.

My husband and I were invited by the Friendship Association to take part in and contribute to the celebrations by sharing our research findings in a seminar organized by the filmmaker Tamara Sushko. Tamara was born in Siberia, but she and her husband, Sergei, have lived in Boden, outside Luleå, for many years among this community of Russian émigrés. In 2015, I was working with her on the script of what would become *Scissors and Secrets*, a documentary film based on the story of Yuri Salnikov. Since its premiere in 2018, *Scissors and Secrets* has won many prizes at film festivals across Russia, from Murmansk to Sevastopol.

Tamara's seminar included a screening of another of her documentary films, *The Children and Prisoners of War from World War II until Today,* and my husband and I gave a presentation of our research work tracing Yuri's birthplace to the fish factory outside Bodø.

Another guest from Norway was daughter-in-law Elena and granddaughter Lisa. Elena Badanina was born in Arkhangelsk on the shores of the Barents Sea but now lives in Narvik, where she works at the Narvik War Museum. Crossing paths with Elena in Luleå was a delightful example of serendipity, for soon after the meeting she was able to fill in some missing information about the military service of Yuri's father, Fedor (see chapter 3). Margareta Söderström, a native of Luleå who was six years old in 1945, shared her memories of the Soviet prisoners. She remembered women and children housed in the schoolhouse at Karlsvik and recalled that she had been encouraged to give a doll to one of the children.

Poster for Secrets and Scissors *(Photo: Tamara Sushko.)*

But the main guests of honor at the event were two of the children born in Norway to imprisoned laborers from the Soviet Union during the late war years: Yuri Salnikov and Valentina Stepina.

Yuri had driven to Luleå, via Bodø, from St. Petersburg with his son Mikhail (the young man we first met in the Stroganov Palace gift shop in 2005), daughter-in-law Lisa, and granddaughter Elena. Since discovering his birthplace, Yuri has returned to Bodø many times, but this was the first visit for his son and family. Valentina's birth in Norway is officially acknowledged, but Yuri is still waiting for the authorities in St. Petersburg to recognize his true birthplace. He now has questions about his citizenship. Having been born in Norway in 1944, is he, in fact, a Norwegian citizen? Or is he Russian? He likes Bodø and hopes to purchase a home in the area.

The other guest of honor was Valentina, daughter of Marfa Stepina. This journey to Luleå was her first trip outside the former Soviet Union. She had come a long way from Bryansk—first by Aeroflot to St. Petersburg, then by train through Helsinki, across Finland to the border town of Haparanda at the top of the Bothnian Gulf, and finally to Luleå. Her plane ticket was paid for by the Russian state under an arrangement that allowed World War II veterans to travel free of charge within Russia during the May anniversary. Sputnik also contributed to the journey.

This was our first meeting with Valentina. Unlike Yuri, she was unable to travel west into Norway to visit Bodø and Langstranda. However, Yuri and Valentina used their meeting in Sweden to exchange stories and memories for the first time. They discovered that during the time they had been in transit in June–July 1945, both had stayed with their mothers in the yellow schoolhouse in Karlsvik, where women with infants were housed. Now they were together in Luleå at a gathering where they were celebrated as guests of honor.

Valentina would be able to take memories of this meeting home with her—to her mother, Marfa Stepina, and to her neighbor and friend Nadezda Lukatina, who had also been born at Frostfilet. Nadezda would learn that their wartime births and early lives were now part of official history—and no longer forgotten, at least in Sweden.

Karlsvik Memories

The unveiling of the monument in Karlsvik served to highlight this forgotten part of Scandinavia's wartime history. A guided tour of Karlsvik and neighboring Karlshäll reminded us how important their docks and warehouses were to Germany's war effort. The Luleå area was a hub thanks to its railroad and port, and German ships transporting men and equipment frequently docked there during the ice-free months. Skirting the shore of the Bothnian Gulf at the northernmost end of the Baltic Sea, the warehouses were used by the Third Reich as a supply and storage center for their military forces in North Norway and Northern Finland from 1940 to 1945. The port was also vital to the export of Swedish iron ore, on which the Third Reich's war industry relied.

On this day in May 2015, we also visited the railway museum, a resting place for old rolling stock, heavy equipment, and memories of railway life, including during wartime. The oldest railroad car dated from 1873. These cars have been used in the making of many films in Norrbotten in the postwar era. Among the handcars was Sweden's only ambulance handcar, which was used until the highway was built between Kiruna and Narvik.

One year after this commemorative gathering, on June 25, 2016, the warehouses burned to the ground. The buildings were still known as the German warehouses.

The Memorial Stone

About 300 people gathered on this Saturday to commemorate the events of the summer of 1945. They included Luleå citizens, Russians, and other immigrants who had built their lives in the area. There were also official representatives of the Swedish and Russian governments in attendance, including the Russian ambassador to Sweden, and representatives from the Murmansk Duma in northern Russia, the Luleå commune, and Karlsvik's Chamber of Commerce.

Volunteers served hot pea soup and pierogies (dumplings). Russian music played as conversations in numerous languages rose above the pine trees surrounding the memorial. Swedish-born Luleå citizens with memories of the events of 1945 mingled with Russians and other immigrants. Some eyewitnesses from 1945 were in their eighties and had themselves been only children at the time. But the experience—and the many stories told about it over the years—remained with them. They spoke of the music, the singing and dancing Russians they had first encountered at the end of the war, and the Soviet mothers with their children in the schoolhouse who had also stayed in their memories.

We gathered in a circle around the monument. Father Vitaly from the Russian Orthodox church in Luleå opened the ceremony with a prayer, after which Katerina Ekstrøm and a representative of Luleå's government unveiled the monument. The writer and historian Lars Gyllenhaal placed the event and ceremony in historical perspective: Lars shared the story of Mikhail Afanasjevitj Gradusov, who had spent four years as a prisoner of war in a Finnish camp. Mikhail said he did not hate his supposed enemies and was, in fact, grateful for the way the Finns had treated him during his captivity. Lars Gyllenhaal declared the core of this message to be: "Do not hate."

The following day, a few hundred people gathered in front of the city hall in the center of Luleå for a peace march. Mostly Russian immigrants and Swedish friends, the participants in our little march walked down Luleå's main street to the "Yellow Pavilion" where we commemorated the end of the war with speeches and songs.

Operation Asphalt and Its Aftermath of Silence

The creation in Sweden of a monument to the Soviet citizens imprisoned in Norway during World War II posed a question: where are the monuments in Norway itself? The answer—there is none—has no single explanation, being rooted in the complex strands of what the historian Steinar Aas calls "memory politics" (see chapter 1). But Operation Asphalt, a little-known aspect of Norway's postwar history, is a key part of understanding why so little remains to physically mark this story.

We have already discussed what is known about the approximately 100,000 prisoners of war and forced laborers who were transported to Norway, and about those who were returned to the Soviet Union after the war ended. The lack of monuments to them is striking in itself, but perhaps even more surprising is the lack of physical memorials for those who never returned, having died during their exile.

During the war, the dead prisoners were buried in graves in many places in Norway, often close to the camps, with memorials constructed by their fellow prisoners. In 1951, with the Cold War now uppermost in the minds of policymakers, the government decided that around 8,000 Soviet prisoners of war should be moved from graves at local sites and placed in common graves. Planning for Operation Asphalt had already begun in 1948, but the digging up and removal of the bodies took place in 1951, during the Korean War, when international tensions were particularly high. The graves were exhumed in two hundred different locations—ninety-five of them in the three northern counties. Bodies from Finnmark, Troms, and Nordland were moved to Tjøtta War Cemetery on the Helgeland coast in Nordland. The operation was code-named Operation Asphalt because the exhumed bodies were transported in asphalt bags.

In the autumn of 1951, two ships sailed from place to place along the coast to carry out the work. The crews usually went ashore at night, excavated the bodies, transported them back to the ship, and moved on to the next graveyard. The destruction of memorials and the secrecy of the excavation work rendered locals in northern Norway horrified spectators of these macabre events. Protests and demonstrations in many towns indicate the strong individual sympathy among Norwegians toward the memory of the Soviet prisoners who died in Norway. But the operation also led to a weakening of the collective memory of the prisoners. Perhaps the darkest aspect of this operation was that the cemeteries—with names, symbols, and monuments made by the prisoners themselves—were systematically destroyed by demolition teams. The silencing was methodical and absolute. Even so, graves of dead soldiers are still found by historically minded Norwegians around the remains of old prison camps.

The policy of erasure and oblivion appears to have shifted after the fall of the Berlin Wall in 1989. Renewed research interest in the field has created new knowledge. Once again, the work of Marianne Neerland Soleim, who provided many clues in our search for Yuri's birthplace (see chapter 2), has been invaluable, most notably in her magisterial 2017 book, *"Operation Asphalt": Cold War and War Graves.*

Yuri's Dream

There is no memorial in Bodø to commemorate the many prisoners of war who were there during those long war years—specifically, the

Soviet women who worked in the fish factories. As elsewhere, historical memorials in Bodø are mainly statues of men. These sculptures stand close to city hall, where they are sheltered from the strong winds of Norway's northern coast.

Yuri, in his capacity as an artist and sculptor, wants to create a memorial with his own hands: a statue of a woman. His desire to honor this missing history reflects what he has learned about his mother, Galina, since our chance meeting with his son Mikhail in St. Petersburg, and what he has seen during his travels to his birthplace. But some of it comes from earlier, fragmented memories of his mother, who died in 1992. He remembers the pain she felt in her hands for as long as she lived, and he surmises that this was caused by the ice-cold water from the conveyor belts that brought fish for filleting.

He recalls trying to question her once, after his uncle Mikhail had let slip the secret of the scissors Galina brought back from Norway (see chapter 2), but he never received satisfactory answers. "The topic was forbidden in the family," he told an interviewer in 2021. Yet she did break her silence a few times later in life. Yuri remembers, "Once, when I was an adult and already knew that I was born in Norway, I asked my mother why they didn't stay there, because Norway is a prosperous country today." Her answer was that she dreamed only of returning home. Sometimes, Galina added, she and other prisoners would walk down to the seashore and gaze into the distance for a long time. But that was as much as she would share with her son about her time in Norway.

Today, having been to Bodø, Yuri is able to reflect on what Galina and the other women would have seen and felt during those long years. "When I got there," he says, "I understood that perhaps the most terrible thing for them was the complete uncertainty. How long would the war last? Would they be liberated? Would they return home?" Though Bodø's coastline can be beautiful, with sunlight sparkling on the waves, he has also seen with his own eyes how it would often have appeared to Galina and her compatriots, given their desperate circumstances: "A gloomy landscape, stones, ruins, and a cold wind."

The weather is a central force anywhere you go, with specific characteristics in different parts of the world. What characterizes the north of Norway is the profound change from summer to winter—summers beneath the midnight sun and winters of total darkness. Bodø and the Lofoten Islands are surrounded by magnificent mountains that invite rain and wind blowing in from the Arctic Ocean. The strong wind must have been an enemy to the prisoners at Frostfilet on their walks from the prison camp in the mornings and back from the factories in the evenings, as well as in their damp and drafty work areas.

Model of Woman in the Wind. *(Photo: Yuri Salnikov.)*

With his artist's eye, Yuri has been working on an idea based on his mother's experience ever since he first visited Bodø. When we met in Luleå in 2015, he brought with him a drawing of a sculpture he envisioned: *The Woman in the Wind*—a tall female figure, her gown and hair blowing in the wind, which he hopes to donate to the city. The completed sculpture, for which he has created a model, would be cast in bronze and stand 2.5 meters high.

There seems to have been a broad agreement in the region and elsewhere that *Woman in the Wind* would make an important statement, both about the war-torn past and the dream of a peaceful future. The well-known Art Foundry in Yekaterinburg, Russia, has agreed to cast the sculpture, and war veterans from the former Soviet Union have pledged to provide financial support. Bodø's mayor approved the idea in May 2015, as did his successor in 2018 when we launched the original edition of this book there. Turning this dream into reality in Bodø has proven challenging. In this administrative heart of Nordland County, a bureaucratic headwind seems to have stifled Yuri's vision. The director of the War Museum in Svolvær, William Hakvaag, is also engaged in finding a place for this memorial in Svolvær.

One day, *Woman in the Wind* will provide a dignified memorial to the many prisoners of war who were brought to Nordland County. But especially, it will preserve the memory of women like Galina, Marfa, and Anny, torn far from their home to work in the fish factories, whose stories were silenced for so long.

AFTERWORD

The telling of this story has been like stitching together a patchwork quilt. Our research took us not only to northern Norway but to Germany, Sweden, and Russia to interview war-time survivors, explore archives and museums, and to walk the streets and landscapes where the events occurred.

Finding traces of women prisoners and the children born to prisoners proved particularly difficult. Their births were not recorded in hospitals, nor in national birth registries or in church parish registries. In some places like Bodø and Narvik where we had hoped to find answers, archives from the war were scarce or non-existent. The museum in Hammerfest would not give us access. But with persistence came successes, small and large. For example, customs manifests and transport declarations that somehow survived over the decades in the archives in Trondheim provided unexpected material, including further proof of historic Nazi–Norwegian collaboration in the fishing industry.

As time passed, we stitched more pieces into the quilt, and a broader picture began to emerge. Photographs, the camp inmate lists from Langstranda, and letters in private and public archives were essential in solving many mysteries. So were interviews with private individuals, some of them deeply engaged in remembering those years. With every new insight into the story's complexities came a sense of triumph.

The more I learned during my research, the more I came to see a central issue—or perhaps more accurately, a central contradiction: the Nazi occupiers' use of Soviet women as slave labor in the Norwegian fishing industry *despite* Nazism's general worldview that women's proper role was to be baby-breeders and homemakers. It was striking to me that this extreme version of "biology is destiny" continued to be reflected in gender relations after the war, continuing to relegate women to tasks related to caring for men and children. I became increasingly aware that the Cold War had actually served to silence discussion about the Nazi views on women and on their place in society vis-à vis men, not only in Norway but across the world. Why had there not been a stronger reckoning with Nazism's supposedly "scientific" views on gender and humanity, not to mention its racism, contempt for weakness, obsession with eugenics, and implementation of sterilization practices and birth-control politics?

Fortunately, the decades following the heyday of the Cold War saw the entry of women into the research world and, with it, widespread questioning of the established "truths" in research, science, and politics. While the classic analyses of Karl Marx and Adam Smith underpinned our early understanding of "men's work" versus the activities of women and children during industrialization, the 1960s and 1970s witnessed the arrival of strong female voices in science, social debates, and political life, notably the sociologist Dorothy E. Smith with her trenchant criticism of hegemonic patriarchal social science. At the same time, voices like Philip Corrigan promoted comparative historical sociology (i.e., studies of the past to understand the future), taking people's experiences as a point of departure in this complex world of ideological struggles.

Among many other insights, such work showed how prevailing ideas about the place of women at any given time responded to the needs of the labor market. The industrial labor market is always in flux, with new technology continuously changing labor processes and resulting in both complexity and conundrums. It was this insight that explained the conundrum at the heart of this book, and brought the various threads and pieces of the patchwork quilt together. In the fish factories of northern Norway, the Nazi ideal of women, tied by biology to *Kinder, Kirche, Küchen* (children, church, kitchen—see chapter 8), was trumped by the needs of a war economy, just as in the post-war Western World, the "ideal" of men at work and women at home was trumped by growing economies' need for new sources of labor to serve new forms of production

I hope others will continue in this field of research, and continue the search in Russia, Belarus, and the Ukraine for former Soviet prisoners and the children who were born to them in Norway during the war. Many people are still in search of their identities.

ACKNOWLEDGMENTS

Yuri Salnikov, the "spark" of this story, developed from being a source in 2005 to almost a co-researcher. As the archives in St. Petersburg have become more open since 2000, Yuri has found valuable new material that sheds light on his history. His smile and happiness upon discovering his birthplace have been huge sources of inspiration for writing this book. I thank him, his wife Natalya, their son Mikhail, and their family for their hospitality and friendship over the years.

There are many others to thank, beginning with the late poet and writer Dag Skogheim, who encouraged me from the very beginning of this work in 2005, and generously shared his knowledge and networks. Born in 1928, and a child of World War II, his background has influenced both his fiction and nonfiction. He lived in Levanger near the Falstad Centre, which was used as an SS camp during the war. Today, it serves as Norway's national center for education and documentation of the history of imprisonment during World War II. We visited the center with Yuri and Natalya during our trip through Norway in 2008, where we had a memorable meeting with Dag Skogheim and historian Marianne Neerland Soleim.

We had come from Bodø, where we had been official guests for three days. I am very grateful to Mayor Kirsten Hasvoll and Sigbjørn Eriksen, the head of Nordland County, for the invitation and for organizing the meetings. We had a memorable time in Bodø. We gave a talk at the University of Bodø with the former director of the National Aviation Museum, Knut Støre, whose archives provided the documents that were key to solving the mystery of Yuri Salnikov's birthplace. We gathered at the art gallery of Oscar Bodøgård and his son Harald, where we met "time witnesses" from the war. One of them was Arne Nystad, a good storyteller, who vividly described the last days in the Langstranda prison camp and in Nordland County on May 8–9, 1945.

Another "time witness" was Torbjørn Feiring, who shared his memories from the last days of the war at Langstranda and has never forgotten the Soviet prisoners' choir and the Russian songs that filled the air. Thanks to Martinius Hauglid, Svein Lundestad, Geir Mortensen, Elisabeth Nilsen, Stig Olsen, Frode Ketil Pettersen, Jarle Sjøvoll, and Ola H. Sæther, who shared their memories and knowledge of the war. Thanks also to Karl Erik Brekke, who in 2008 opened the premises of Frostfilet A/S for a tour, and gave one of the original bricks, marked "Frostfilet," as a gift to Yuri Salnikov.

Marfa Maksimovna Stepina and Anny Evensen, who had both worked at the factories, were important witnesses from the war years. Nadelzda Lakutina and Valentina Stepina who, like Yuri, were born at Langstranda, shared memories of their mothers and of the bitter reality of growing up "under a cloud" in the USSR. Maria Maksimovna Stepina, Nadelzda Lakutina, and Valentina Stepina were interviewed by the Russian Swedish filmmaker Tamara Sushko in her film *Karlsvik: On the Way Home* (2013), which was a huge inspiration in my understanding of everyday life at Langstranda. I've had a rich relationship with Tamara, which led to the documentary film *Scissors and Secrets*, based on this book. I also thank her for hosting us in Luleå several times, and for our friendship over the years. In 2015, we met and interviewed Valentina Stepina in her home, with Tamara serving as an interpreter.

From the Norwegian communities who involuntarily "hosted" the Soviet forced laborers, I thank William Hakvaag at the Lofoten War Memorial Museum in Svolvær for his extraordinary dedication to the project. He is collaborating with us to create a space at Svinøya for Yuri's sculpture, *Woman in the Wind*. He also arranged contact with Erling Johan Nilsen, who had worked with the women from Hammerfest at Svinøya in 1944–45. We spent two days with him and greatly benefited from his clear recollections. Thank you. I also thank Roald Hansen in Melbu in Vesterålen for sharing his knowledge about the Fredriksen fish factory.

There has been enormous generosity from researchers in the field. Thanks to curator Dag Andreassen of the Norwegian Museum of Science and Technology, Professor Hans Petter Finstad and Professor Marianne Neeland Soleim of The Arctic University of Norway, the writer Knut Støre in Bodø, and Dr. Michael Stokke of the Narvik Museum of War. The journalist Per Jevne has also been a great supporter. They have all contributed their knowledge and shared their archives.

Nordland Museum contributed pictures from their collections. Thanks to Oscar Berg and Petter Snekkerstad from the Nordland Museum, as well as to Audun Spjell from Bodø's War History Museum, Ivar Dyb Kroglund from the Home Front Museum in Oslo, and Jan Bergsten from the Norrbotten Railroad Museum in Karlsvik. A special thanks goes to Elena Badanina of the Narvik War Museum, who managed to find new information about Yuri's father, Fedor Salnikov, in the Russian archives. Curator Lyudmila Guseva was our guide at the Y. A. Gagarin Museum in Gzhatsk, which featured a major exhibit on the fate of this small town during World War II. She and the other curator showed great interest in the new information, as they had not previously known of the story of the children born in Norway of Soviet parents during the war.

Germany is one of the leading countries in both archives and research on the history of forced labor during WWII. I thank Dr. Reinhard Otto, who lives in Eastern Westphalia, for his research and help with archives, and Dr. Robert Bohn from Flensburg University for his inspiring work on male and female forced labor in Norway. Roland Masslich and Hans-Jürgen Kahle in Cuxhaven, Germany, have generously shared their archives and empirical work on the Norwegian fish industry during the war.

The late Dr. Gisela Schwarze's important work on "Ostarbeiterinnen und ihre Kinder im Zweiten Weltkrieg" ("Women Workers from the East and Their Children in World War II"), which explores women slave laborers and their children during the war, was central to my research and understanding of Nazi practices and ideology regarding the contradictions in their treatment of "Women from the East" and "Norwegian Women."

The central question that has occupied me for many years is the Nazi view on the importance of Norwegian women as so-called Aryan baby-breeders for the Third Reich, along with the children they gave birth to in Norway during the war. I greatly benefited from the work of two women, the late Professor Daša Drndić from Croatia and Professor Despina Stratigakos from the USA. Both have studied these matters extensively as they occurred in Norway, a country far from their homelands. Their thorough work, on both what happened and the ideas behind it, has provided new insight into these complex questions.

Archivists and librarians have helped me find the path toward new knowledge. The archivists in Trondheim were especially helpful in the project. Many thanks to Andre Bialk, chief librarian at Oslo Metropolitan University, for his knowledge and help in finding important material that has enriched the book. I also thank Ingeborg M. Andersen, Rainer Hoppe, Lars Gyllenhaal, Alexey Kyrylenko, and Laila Thorsen for their conversations and contributions.

Friends and colleagues, both old and new, have supported and encouraged me through good and dark times. Swedish filmmaker Gunilla Breski has been with me throughout the process of creating the English version, sharing her knowledge from Russia and inspiring my writing. She made the first documentary film about Soviet prison camps in northern Norway, titled *Blodveien* (*The Blood Road*) (2000). Wennicke Eide Cox, Toril Hanssen, Bibbi Lee, Tora Margot Ørstad, and Michael Seltzer have stood by my side since the beginning, and have provided invaluable support along the way. Svein Sandnes contributed valuable editing assistance and helped provide the final punctuation mark to the Norwegian version.

Bibbi Lee completed the first translation from Norwegian to English in 2019. Since then, the book has been revised many times. Sofia Karas, a graduate student in Russian Studies, came from London to Oslo at a critical stage in August 2023 and we worked on the book together using her fresh views and critical ideas. It was a lovely collaboration.

Thanks also to Humphrey Hawksley and Jan-Gustav Strandenaes for independently reviewing the manuscript. Special thanks to Michael Springer who sensitively and expertly copyedited the final text. We also thank International Mapping for helping the reader locate the story in geographical space.

This publication would never have happened without the enthusiasm and support of my editors Judy Blankenship and Andrew Wilson. Andrew has been an invaluable partner, researching, editing, and adding wider dimensions to this version, and updating the story into the times we are living now. Judy Blankenship has been a friend, editor, and supporter for more than five decades and across (at least) three continents. She encouraged this English version of the book from the beginning.

As always, my husband, Richard, has provided constant, loving support through this and so many other adventures.

Tusen takk! Спасибо. Thank you all!

BIBLIOGRAPHY

Aas, Steinar. "Norwegian and Soviet/Russian World War II Memory Policy During the Cold War and the Post-Soviet Years." *Acta Borealia* 29, no. 2 (2012): 211–31. https://doi.org/10.1080/08003831.2012.678721.

Abraham, Ole-Jacob. "Russarfangene—mytar, fakta og nyanser" ["Russian Prisoners: Myths, Facts, and Nuances"]. *Historisk Tidsskrift*, no. 2 (2009).

Ahuja, Ishita, et al. "Fish- and Fish-Waste-Based Fertilizers in Organic Farming—With Status in Norway: A Review." *Waste Management* 115 (2020): 95–112. https://doi.org/10.1016/j.wasman.2020.07.025.

Alexievich, Svetlana. *The Unwomanly Face of War: An Oral History of Women in World War II*. Translated by Richard Pevear and Larissa Volokhonsky. Penguin, 2017.

Alexievich, Svetlana. *Secondhand Time: The Last of the Soviets*. Translated by Bela Shayevich. Random House, 2016.

Alexopoulos, Golfo. "Amnesty 1945: The Revolving Doors of Stalin's Gulag." *Slavic Review* 64, no. 2 (2005): 274–306.

Anatoli, A. *Babi Yar: A Document in the Form of a Novel*. Sphere Books, 1970.

Andreassen, Dag. *Kjøle og fryseteknologi: fra planer til industri. Den norsk-tyske filetfabrikk på Melbu 1940–45* [*Cooling and Freezer Technology from Plans to Industry: The Norwegian–German Fish-Fillet Plant at Melbu 1940–45*]. Universitetet i Bergen, 1995.

Applebaum, Anne. *Iron Curtain: The Crushing of Eastern Europe, 1944–1956*. Penguin, 2012.

Ascherson, Neil. "After Seven Hundred Years." *London Review of Books*, May 24, 2012, 7–8.

Bellamy, Chris. *Absolute War: Soviet Russia in World War II*. Pan Macmillan, 2007.

Berezhkov, Valentin. *History in the Making: Memoirs of World War II Diplomacy*. Progress Publishers, 1982.

Bohn, Robert. "Zwangsarbeiter und Zwangsarbeiterinnen im Reichskommissariat Norwegen: Fakten und Erinnerung" ["Male and Female Forced Labor in Germany's Norwegian Reichskommissariat: Facts and Memories"]. In *Zwangsarbeit in Hitlers Europa: Besatzung—Arbeit—Folgen* [*Forced Labor in Hitler's Europe: Occupation—Work—Consequences*], edited by Dieter Pohl and Tanja Sebta. Metropol, 2013.

Borgen, P. H. F., and T. Hofsbro. *Norske polititropper i Sverige/Norge 1943–45: Operasjone i Norge 1944–1945* [*Norwegian Police Troops in Sweden/Norway 1943–45: Operations in Norway 1944–1945*]. Veteranforeningens historielag,

2006.
Borkin, Joseph, and Charles A. Welsh. *Germany's Master Plan: The Story of Industrial Offensive*. Duell, Sloan & Pearce, 1943.
Braseth, Ann-Cathrin, and Astrid Borchgrevink Lund. "Sendt til fiendens leir" ["Sent into the Enemy Camp"]. In *About Bodø*. Bodø Municipality, 1991.
Bridenthal, Renate, Atina Grossmann, and Marion Kaplan, eds. *When Biology Became Destiny: Women in Weimar and Nazi Germany.* Monthly Review Press, 1984.
Buruma, Ian. *Year Zero: A History of 1945*. Atlantic Books, 2013.
Callill, Carmen. *Bad Faith: A Story of Family and Fatherland.* Vintage, 2007.
Christie, Nils. *Fangevoktere i konsentrasjonsleire* [*Prison Guards in Concentration Camps*]. Pax Forlag, 1972.
Clodfelter, Michael. *Warfare and Armed Conflicts: A Statistical Reference to Casualty and Other Figures, 1500–2000.* 2nd ed. McFarland, 2001.
Corrigan, Philip. *Social Forms/Human Capacities (RLE Social Theory): Essays in Authority and Difference*. Routledge, 2020.
Cottam, Kazimiera. *Women in War and Resistance: Selected Biographies of Soviet Women Soldiers*. Focus, 1998.
Cullum, Linda. "Whose Interest? Women Organizing on the Waterfront—St Johns, Newfoundland." *Journal of Historical Sociology* 22, no. 1 (2009): 71–96.
Dahl, Hans Fredrik, ed. *Krigen i Norge* [*The War in Norway*]. Pax Forlag, 1974.
de Waal, Alex. "The Nazis Used It; We Use It." *London Review of Books*, June 14, 2017. https://www.lrb.co.uk/the-paper/v39/n12/alex-de-waal/the-nazis-used-it-we-use-it.
Drndić, Daša. *Trieste*. Houghton Mifflin Harcourt, 2012.
Eidum, Espen. *Blodsporet: Sveriges bidrag til naziokkupasjonen av Norge* [*Trail of Blood: Sweden's Contribution to the Nazi Occupation of Norway*]. Kristiansen Forlag, 2012.
Emberland, Terje, and Matthew Kott. *Himmlers Norge: Nordmenn i det storgermanske prosjekt* [*Himmler's Norway: Norwegians in the Greater-Germanic Project*]. Aschehoug, 2012.
Eriksson, Kjersti, ed. *Women and War in Norway and Beyond.* Routledge, 2016.
Finstad, Bjørn Petter. "The Norwegian Fishing Sector during the German Occupation: Continuity or Change?" In *Industrial Collaboration in Nazi-Occupied Europe: Norway in Context*, edited by Hans Otto Frøland, Mats Ingulstad, and Jonas Scherner, 389–415. Palgrave Macmillan, 2016. https://doi.org/10.1057/978-1-137-53423-1_15.
Finstad, Bjørn Petter. "Spiskammer for det tredje riket" ["Larders for the Third Reich"]. In *Norges fiskeri og kysthistorie* [*The Norwegian Fishery and Coastal History*], edited by Nils Kolle et al. Akademisk Forlag, 2014.
Finstad, Bjørn Petter. "The Norwegian Fisheries during the German Occupation: Change and Continuity." In *Fish, War and Politics in the North-Atlantic Fisheries, 1300–2003*, edited by F. R. Loomeier et al. Studia Atlantica/Netwerk

15, 2004.

Finstad, Bjørn Petter. "Hanna Anny from the Ukraine—A Pioneer in the Fishing Industry of Northern Norway." In *Global Coasts: Life Changes, Gender Challenges*, edited by Siri Gerrard and Randi Rønning Balsvik, 30–38. Kvinnforsk Occasional Papers. University of Tromsø, 1999.

Finstad, Bjorn Petter. *Fiskerinæringen i Finnmark under okkupasjonen* [*The Fishing Industry in Finnmark During the Occupation*]. Unpublished MA thesis, University of Tromsø, 1993.

Fløgstad, Kjartan. *Grense Jakobselv* [*The Jakob River Border*]. Gyldendal Norsk Forlag, 2009.

Frankenberger, Tamara. *Lebensgeschichtliche Bedeutung von Zwangsarbeit* [*Living Memories of Forced Labor*]. Forum Geschichtskultur, Ruhrlandmuseum, 2000.

Frøland, Carl Müller. *Nazimens ideunivers* [*The Nazi Universe of Ideas*]. Vidarforlaget, 2017.

Glucksmann, Miriam. *Women Assemble: Women Workers and the New Industries in Inter-War Britain*. Routledge, 1990.

Gogstad, Anders. "50 års minne, sett fra den andre siden: En tysk kollegas inntrykk fra sine år i Norge som militærlege 1940–1945" ["50 Years of Memory, Seen from the Other Side: A German Colleague's Impressions of His Years in Norway as a Military Doctor, 1940–45"]. *Tidsskrift for Den norske legeforening* 115, no. 30 (1995): 3765–67.

Grønlie, Rune. "Foreldrene var fanger i Bodø" ["Their Parents Were Prisoners in Bodø"]. *Avisa Nordland*, September 24, 2008.

Grossman, Vasily. *Stalingrad*. Random House, 2019.

Grossman, Vasily. *A Writer at War: Vasily Grossman with the Red Army 1941–1945*. Edited and translated by Antony Beevor and Luba Vinogradova. Pimlico/Random House, 2006.

Grytås, Gunnar. *Malmtunge spor: Historia om Ofotbanen* [*Heavy Tracks of Iron Ore: History of the Ofot Railway*]. Det Norske Samlaget, 2017.

Grytås, Gunnar. *Motmakt og samfunnsbygger: Med torsken og Norges Råfisklag gjennom 75 år* [*Countering Power and Building Society: Seventy-Five Years with Norway's Cod and Raw Fish Sector*]. Akademika Forlag, 2013.

Guhnfeldt, Cato. "Lofotraidet fikk et uventet utbytte" ["Unexpected Payoff to the Lofot Raid"]. *Aftenposten*, March 16, 2016.

Gyllenhaal, Lars. "Röda armén i Sverige" ["The Red Army in Sweden"]. *Populär Historia*, no. 6 (2016).

Gyllenhaal, Lars, and James F. Gebhardt. *Slaget om Nordkalotten* [*The Battle for Nordkalotten*]. Historiska Media, 1999.

Hagen, Thomas V. H. "Nordmenn i fangenskap under andre verdenskrig" ["Norwegians in Captivity during World War II"]. In *Nordmenn i fangenskap 1940–1945*. Universitetsforlaget, 2004.

Hakvaag, William. *De utrolige bildene* [*Unbelievable Pictures*]. Kolofon Forlag, 2013.

Hatlehol, Gunnar D. "Prisoners and Forced Laborers in German-Occupied Norway, 1940–1945: A Historiographical Survey." *Arbeiderhistorie* 24, no. 1 (2020): 61–83.

Hatlehol, Gunnar D. *"Norwegeneinsatz" 1940–1945: Organisation Todts arbeidere i Norge og graden av tvang* [*"The Norwegian Effort," 1940–1945: Organisation Todt's Workers in Norway and Degrees of Coercion*]. NTNU, 2015.

Haugland, Magne. *Do Svidania—På gjensyn: Dokumentarberetninger om sovjetiske krigsfanger* [*Do Svidania—Goodbye: Documented Accounts of Soviet Prisoners of War*]. Commentum Forlag, 2008.

Haukland, Linda Helen. *Hverdag i ruinene* [*Ruins of Everyday Life*]. Orkana Akademisk, 2012.

Haukland, Linda Helen. *Bodø under andre verdenskrig: Narrativ og faktuell tilnærming til muntlige kilder* [*Bodø during World War II: Narrative and Factual Approaches to Oral Sources*]. Master's thesis, Høgskolen i Bodø, 2010.

Helskog, Anne. *Det er bombevær i natt: Fire år i Festung Kirkenes* [*It's Bombing Weather Tonight: Four Years in Fortress Kirkenes*]. Bealljecohkka, 2006.

Hitler, Adolf. *Mein Kampf.* Houghton Mifflin, 1943.

Hjeltnes, Guri. "Fangeskipet 'Donau's' siste reis" ["The Final Voyage of Prison Ship Donau"]. *Aftenposten,* April 9, 2014.

Hunt, Karen. *The World Transformed, 1914–1945.* Pearson, 2014.

Husmo, Marit. "Gender and Total Quality Management: The Quality Assurance Process in Norwegian Fish Processing." In *Global Coasts: Life Changes, Gender Challenges*, edited by Siri Gerrard and Randi Rønning Balsvik, 11–19. Kvinnforsk Occasional Papers. University of Tromsø, 1999.

Jacobsen, Alf R. *Hat. Hevn. Håp: Historien om det moderne Norge 1945–2000* [*Hate. Revenge. Hope: The History of Modern Norway 1945–2000*]. Vega Forlag, 2015.

Jacobsen, Alf R. *Miraklet ved Lista: Hitlers første nederlag på Østfronten* [*Miracle at Lista: Hitler's First Defeat on the Eastern Front*]. Vega Forlag, 2014.

Jacobsen, Alf R. *Fra brent jord til Klondyke* [*From Scorched Earth to Klondike*]. Universitetsforlaget, 1996.

Jaklin, Asbjørn. *Brent jord 1944–1945: Heltene, ofrene, de skyldige* [*Scorched Earth 1944–45: The Heroes, the Victims, the Guilty*]. Gyldendal, 2016.

Jentoft, Morten. *Mennesker ved en grense: En beretning om folk i Øst-Finnmark i historiens drama* [*People on a Border: An Account of the Historical Drama of the People of East Finnmark*]. Gyldendal, 2006.

Kahle, Hans Jürgen. *Verschleppt nach Cuxhaven: Eine Dokumentation über das Schicksal der ausländischen Arbeiter und Kriegsgefangenen in Cuxhaven, im Kreis Land Hadeln und dem Landkreis Wesermünde während der Zeit des Nationalsozialismus* [*Carried Away into the Cuxhaven Night: Documenting the Fate of Foreign Workers and Prisoners of War in Cuxhaven, Kreis Land Hadeln*

Province, and Wesermünde (Bremerhaven) during the Time of National Socialism]. Wilhelm-Heidsiek Verlag, 1995.

Karol, K. S. *Solik: Life in the Soviet Union, 1939–1946*. Pluto Press, 1983.

Kitchen, Martin. *Speer: Hitler's Architect*. Yale University Press, 2015.

Kleve, Karl L. *The Many Faces of the Cold War*. Norwegian Aviation Museum, 1999.

Kolle, Nils, et al. *Norges fiskeri og kysthistorie* [*Norway's Fishery and Coastal History*]. Akademisk Forlag, 2014.

Koonz, Claudia. *Mothers in the Fatherland: Women, the Family, and Nazi Politics*. St. Martin's Press, 1987.

Korsnes, Eivind, and Johan Sira. *Sør-Varanger: Fangeleirer og andre typer leirer og fengsler i tiden 1940–44* [*South Varanger: Prisoner Camps and Other Types of Camps and Prisons between 1940–44*]. Sør-Varanger Museum, 2012.

Kozhemyakina, Olga. "'Я родился в немецком плену' …" ["I Was Born in German Captivity …"]. *Pravmir.ru*, March 10, 2020. https://www.pravmir.ru/ya-rodilsya-v-nemeczkom-plenu-ob-etom-arhitektor-iz-peterburga-uznal-cherez-50-let/.

Kreyberg, Leiv. *Frigjøringen av de allierte krigsfangene i Nordland i 1945: En redegjørelse* [*An Account of Freeing the Allies' Prisoners of War in Nordland in 1945*]. Tanum, 1946.

Krog, Helge. *Sjette-kolonne: Om den norske storindustriens bidrag til Nazi-Tysklands krigføring* [*Sixth Column: On the Contribution of Norway's Heavy Industry to Nazi Germany's Warfare*]. Pax, 1969.

Kuczynski, J., and M. Witt. *The Economics of Barbarism: Hitler's New Economic Order in Europe*. Frederick Muller, 1942.

Kurlansky, Mark. *Cod: A Biography of the Fish That Changed the World*. Penguin Putnam, 1998.

Lee, Sabine. *Children Born of War in the Twentieth Century*. Oxford University Press, 2017.

Longerich, Peter. *Heinrich Himmler: A Life*. Oxford University Press, 2011.

Lorentzen, Annemarie. "Fra Ukraina—en gang verdens kornkammer—til verdens nordligste by" ["From Ukraine—Once the World's Grain Silo—to the World's Northernmost City"]. *Øyfolk*, no. 8 (1987). Hammerfest Historielag.

Lower, Wendy. *Hitler's Furies: German Women in the Nazi Killing Fields*. Vintage, 2014.

Magra, Iliana. "Norway Apologizes, 70 Years Later, to Women Who Had Relationships with WWII Germans." *New York Times*, October 19, 2018.

Meaney, Thomas. "So It Must Be Forever." *London Review of Books*, July 14, 2016, 5–7.

Meland, Astrid. "Sjarmert til spionasje" ["Charmed into Espionage"]. *Dagbladet*, April 27, 2004, magasinet section. https://www.dagbladet.no/magasinet/sjarmert-til-spionasje/65961967.

Michelet, Marte B. *Hva visste hjemmefronten? Holocaust i Norge: Varslene, unnvikelsene, hemmeligholdet* [*What Did the Home Front Know? The Holocaust in Norway: The Warnings, the Evasions, the Secrecy*]. Gyldendal, 2018.

Michelet, Marte B. *Den største forbrytelsen: Ofre og gjerningsmenn i det norske Holocaust* [*The Greatest Crime: Victims and Perpetrators in the Norwegian Holocaust*]. Gyldendal, 2014.

Milward, Alan S. "Fascism and the Economy." In *Fascism: A Reader's Guide*, edited by Walter Laqueur. Penguin, 1976.

Milward, Alan S. *The Fascist Economy in Norway.* Clarendon Press, 1972.

Mjelde, Liv. "New Gender Challenges, New Demands." In *Left Feminism in Europe*, edited by Frigga Haug. Argument, 2008.

Mjelde, Liv. "From Factory and Housework to Oil and Caring: Changes in Girls' Education in the Vocational Fields during the Years of Reform '94." In *Gender Perspectives on Vocational Education*, edited by Philipp Gonon et al.. Peter Lang, 2001.

Mjelde, Liv. *Apprenticeship: From Practice to Theory and Back Again.* University of Joensuu, Publications in Social Sciences No. 19, 1993.

Mjelde, Liv. "Kjønn, arbeidsdeling og forandring i den grafiske bedriften" ["Gender, Division of Labor and Change in the Printing Industry"]. In *Arbeidsdeling i en brytningstid*, edited by Liv Mjelde and A. L. Tarrou. Gyldendal, 1992.

Mjelde, Liv. "Between Schooling and Work: Women and Vocational Training in Scandinavia." *Resources for Feminist Research* 13, no. 1 (1984b).

Mjelde, Liv. "Education, Labor Force, the Family: The Connection." *Resources for Feminist Research* 13, no. 1 (1984a).

Mjelde, Liv. "Bygningsarbeid, mannfolk yrke eller?" ["Building Trades, Men's Work, or…?"]. In *Kvinnens årbok* [*Women's Yearbook*]. Pax, 1975.

Moorehead, Caroline. *A Train in Winter: A Story of Resistance, Friendship and Survival in Auschwitz.* Vintage, 2012.

Mosse, George L. *Nazi Culture: Intellectual, Cultural and Social Life in the Third Reich.* Schocken Books, 1981.

Moynahan, Brian. *Leningrad: Siege and Symphony.* Quercus Editions, 2013.

Myles, Bruce. *Night Witches: The Amazing Story of Russia's Women Pilots in World War II.* Panther Books, 1983.

Neegaard, Dan Petter. *Ljudmila Pavlitsjenko: Valhall.* Vega Forlag, 2014.

Nilsen, Bjørn. *Altså egentlig n' Nekolai: historia om oppfinneren, sildegrossisten og originalen Nekolai Dahl* [*Actually, It's n' Nekolai: The Story of the Inventor, Herring Wholesaler and Original Nekolai Dahl*]. Steinbit Forlag, 2006.

Nordhus, Henrik. *Kirkenes i krigsåra 1940–1945. Kirkenes brannvesen og Det sivile luftverns beretning* [*Kirkenes During the War Years 1940–1945. Kirkenes Fire Department and Civil Air Defense Report*]. Sør-Varanger kommune, 1948.

Offen, Karen M. *European Feminisms, 1700–1950: A Political History.* Stanford University Press, 2000.

Ofstad, Harald. *Vår forakt for svakhet: En analyse av nazismens normer og vurderinger* [*Our Contempt for Weakness: An Analysis of the Norms and Evaluations of Nazism*]. Pax, 1971.

Otterstad, Bernt L. "Eugenikkrati (Eugenicracy)." *Klassekampen*, May 13, 2017.

Paris, Erna. *Long Shadows: Truth, Lies and History*. Vintage Canada/Random House, 2001.

Paulsen, Helge. "Tysk økonomisk politikk i Norge 1940–45." In *Krigen i Norge* [*The War in Norway*], edited by Hans Fredrik Dahl. Pax, 1974.

Petterson, Arvid. *Fortiet fortid: Tragedien Norge aldri forsto. Tvangsevakuering og overvintring i Nord-Troms og Finnmark 1944–1945* [*The Concealed Past. Forced Evacuation and Surviving the Winter in North Troms and Finnmark 1944–45*]. Gjenreisningsmuseet for Finnmark og Nord-Troms, 2008.

Phillips, Trevor, and Mike Phillips. *Windrush: Seventy-Five Years of Modern Britain.* Mudlark, 2023.

Polmar, Norman. "Soviet Shipbuilding and Shipyards." *United States Naval Institute Proceedings* 98, no. 5 (1972): 55–63.

Putin, Vladimir V., and Natalya P. Gevorkian. *First Person: An Astonishingly Frank Self-Portrait.* Hutchinson, 2000.

Regis, Ed. *Who Got Einstein's Office?* Addison-Wesley, 1987.

Renan, Ernest. *Qu'est-ce qu'une nation?* [*What Is a Nation?*]. Presses Pocket, 1992.

Riste, Olav, and Berit Nøkleby. *Norway 1940-45: The Resistance Movement.* 3rd ed. Aschehoug, 1994.

Rosenberg, Eva. "Englandsturen" ["Tour of England"]. In *Årbok for Vågan.* Skolp, 2014.

Rybakk, Timothy. *Hitler's First Victims: The Quest for Justice*. Vintage Books, 2015.

Ryeng, Nils, Ole Chr. Føre, and Olav Ravn. *Hemmelig krig i nord: Historien om XU i Nord-Norge* [*Secret War in the North: The History of XU in North Norway*]. Orion Forlag, 2009.

Schmitt, Carl. *The Concept of the Political.* Expanded ed. Edited by George Schwab. University of Chicago Press, 2007.

Schwarze, Gisela. *Ostarbeiterinnen und ihre Kinder im Zweiten Weltkrieg* [*Women Workers from the East and Their Children in World War II*]. Forum Geschichtskultur, Ruhrlandmuseum, 2000.

Service, Robert. *A History of Modern Russia from Nicholas II to Vladimir Putin.* Harvard University Press, 2005.

Skarstein, Atle, and Mikhail Stokke. *Blod og tårer: Historien om sovjetiske krigsfanger og sivile tvangsarbeidere i Rogaland 1941–1945* [*Blood and Tears: The History of Soviet Prisoners of War and Civilian Forced Laborers in Rogaland*]. Commentum Forlag, 2010.

Skarstein, Karl Jakop. *Store slag: Moskva 1941* [*Great Battles: Moscow, 1941*]. Spartacus, 2013.

Skjeseth, Alf. *Nordens Casablanca: Nordmenn i Stockholm under krigen* [*The Casablanca of the North: Norwegians in Stockholm during the War*]. Spartacus, 2018.

Skogheim, Dag. *Med slukte lanterner* [*With Lanterns Snuffed Out*]. Gjenreisningsmuseet for Finnmark og Nord-Troms, 1998.

Skogheim, Dag. *Prolog for markeringen i Falstadskogen 7. mai 1995* [*Prologue for the Commemoration in the Falstad Forest, May 7, 1995*]. Falstad Centre, 1995.

Soleim, Marianne Neerland. "Graves of the 'Other': Norway and the Commemoration of Soviet Prisoners of War." *Heritage, Memory and Conflict* 3 (2023): 15–18. https://doi.org/10.3897/hmc.3.71298.

Soleim, Marianne Neerland. *"Operasjon asfalt": Kald krig om krigsgraver* [*Operation Asphalt: Cold War over War Graves*]. Orkana Akademisk, 2016.

Soleim, Marianne Neerland, Lars-Erik Vaeng, and Per Kristian Skulberg. *Grenseløs i grenseland: Samisk og norsk losvirksomhet i Nordre Nordland og Sør-Troms 1945* [*Without Borders in Borderland: Sámi and Norwegian Piloting in Nordre Nordland and Sør-Troms 1945*]. Orkana Akademisk, 2016.

Soleim, Marianne Neerland. "Female Forced Laborers from 'the East'—A Forgotten Part of Norwegian War History." In *Women in War: Examples from Norway and Beyond*, edited by Kjersti Ericsson. Ashgate Publishing, 2015.

Soleim, Marianne Neerland, Jens-Ivar Nergård, and Oddmund Andersen. *Grenselos i grenseland* [*Borderless in a Borderland*]. Orkana Akademisk, 2015.

Soleim, Marianne Neerland, ed. *Prisoners of War and Forced Labor: Histories of War and Occupation.* Cambridge Scholars Publishing, 2010.

Soleim, Marianne Neerland. *Sovjetiske krigsfanger i Norge 1941–1945: Antall, organisering og repatriering* [*Soviet Prisoners of War in Norway 1941–1945: Numbers, Organization, and Repatriation*]. Spartacus Forlag, 2009.

Soleim, Marianne Neerland. *Sovjetiske krigsfanger i Norge 1941–1945: Antall, organisering og repatriering* [*Soviet Prisoners of War in Norway 1941–1945: Numbers, Organization, and Repatriation*]. PhD diss., University of Tromsø, 2004.

Steffenak, Einar Kr. *Russerfangene: Sovjetiske krigsfanger i Norge og deres skjebne* [*Russian Prisoners: Soviet Prisoners of War in Norway and Their Fate*]. Humanist Forlag, 2008.

Stokke, Michael. *Sovjetiske og franske sivilarbeidere i Norge 1942–1945: En sammenligning av arbeids- og leveforhold* [*Soviet and French Civilian Workers in Norway 1942–45*]. Master's thesis, University of Bergen, 2008.

Storeide, Anette. *Norske krigsprofitører: Nazi-Tysklands velvillige medløpere* [*Norwegian War Profiteers: Nazi Germany's Willing Collaborators*]. Gyldendal, 2014.

Strand, Morten. *St. Petersburg-historier* [*St. Petersburg Stories*]. Tiden Norsk Forlag, 2005.

Stratigakos, Despina. *Hitler's Northern Utopia: Building the New Order in Occupied Norway.* Princeton University Press, 2020.

Strong, Tracy B. Introduction to *The Concept of the Political*, by Carl Schmitt, vii–xlix. University of Chicago Press, 2007.

Tabeling, Petra. "Children of Shame – Norway's Dark Secret." *Deutsche Welle*, December 2 2001. https://www.dw.com/en/children-of-shame-norways-dark-secret/a-336916.

Tamnes, Rolf. *The United States and the Cold War in the High North.* Gower House, 1991.

Thorsen, Laila. *For det daglige brød: Et kystfolks historie* [*For Their Daily Bread: History of a Coastal People*]. Eget Forlag, 1996.

Thorsen, Thor. "Erinnerungen an die Lohmann-fabrik in Hammerfest" ["Memories of the Lohmann Factory in Hammerfest"]. *Trollposten* 6, nos. 2 & 3 (2000).

Trevor-Roper, Hugh. *The Last Days of Hitler.* Macmillan, 1947.

Trondenes Historic Center. "A Soviet Prisoner of War Tells His Story." *Nord Norge*, https://nordnorge.com/en/artikkel/a-soviet-prisoner-of-war-tells-his-story/.

Ulateig, Egil. *Freden: 8. Mai 1945.* 1st ed. Vigmostad & Bjørke, 2015.

Werth, Alexander. *Russia at War, 1941–1945.* Avon Books, 1964.

Westerlund, Lars. "Utländska soldater och unga kvinnor under andra världskriget: Kulturmöten i Västeuropa och råhet i Östeuropa; moderniseringsvånda i Nordfinland och på Island" ["Foreign Soldiers and Young Women during World War II: Cultural Encounter in Western Europe and Brutality in Eastern Europe; the Agony of Modernization in Northern Finland and on Iceland"]. *Tornedalens årsbok*, no. 14 (2011).

Westlie, Bjørn, *Det norske jødehatet: Propaganda og presse under okkupasjonen* [*Norway's Anti-Semitism: Propaganda and Press during the Occupation*]. Res Publica, 2019.

Westlie, Bjørn. *Fangene som forsvant: NSB og slavearbeiderne på Nordlandsbanen* [*Prisoners Who Disappeared: The Norwegian Railway and Slave Laborers on the Nordland Line*]. Spartacus, 2015.

Wormdal, B. "Tyskerbarna fikk erstatning—hvorfor kan ikke vi russerbarn få det?" ["The German Children Got Compensation, Why Can't We Russian Children Get It?"], NRK, August 5, 2020. https://www.nrk.no/tromsogfinnmark/krever-oppreisning-for-russerbarna_-slik-tyskerbarna-fikk-1.15109146

Zemskov, Victor. "Hjemsendelse av sovjetiske borgere og deres skjebne" ["Repatriation of Soviet Citizens and Their Fate"]. *Sociologiskie issledovanija*, no.11, 3–17.

Zetterling, Niclas & Anders Frankson 2013. *Hitlers første nederlag. Slaget om Moskva* [*Hitler's First Defeat: The Battle for Moscow*]. Spartacus, 2013.

Other Sources (Newspapers, Newspaper Articles, Films, Periodicals, Public Annual Report, Lectures, TV Programs)

Aftenposten. May 7, 1945.

Aktuell. "Russerne reiser hjem" ["Russians Journey Home"]. No. 3 (July 14, 1945).

Arbeiderbladet 70 år: Særtrykk 1945 [*70 Years: Special 1945*]. 1945.

Avisa Nordland. May 22, 2015.

Jag stannar tiden [*I Bring Time to a Halt*]. Directed by Gunilla Breski. Luleå, 2014. Documentary film.

Dagsavisen. October 14, 2014.

Dagsavisen. October 18, 2014, 33.

Dagbladet Magasinet. May 2, 2015.

Finnmarks Dagblad. July 11, 1984.

Falstadsenteret. *Ansikt til Ansikt / Face to Face: Utstillingskatalog*. 2007.

Fiskeridirektøren. *Årsberetning vedrørende Lofotfisket*, no. 2. 1945.

Forsvarets forum. 1994.

Fremover. June 25, 1945.

Grønlie, Rune. "Foreldrene var fanger i Bodø" ["Their Parents Were Prisoners in Bodø"]. *Avisa Nordland*, September 24, 2008.

Völkischer Beobachter. September 15, 1935, no. 255; September 13, 1936, no. 257. (Berlin).

Iskyss [*The Ice Kiss*]. Directed by Knut Erik Jensen. Tromsø Film, 2008. Feature film.

Norrländska Socialdemokraten. June 14, 1945.

Norrbotten Kuriren. June 27, 2015.

"Jurij Salnikov. Født i fangeleir på Langstranda" ["Juri Salnikov: Born in a Prisoner-of-War Camp at Langstranda"]. *NRK Nordland*, television broadcast, September 23, 2008.

Oslo-pressen. May 8–12, 1945.

Ofotens Tidende. June 6, 12, and 14, 1945.

Sputnik Info, no. 11 (Luleå, 2015).

Støre, Knut. "Krigsfanger og tvangsarbeidere i Bodø under 2. verdenskrig" ["Prisoners of War and Forced Laborers in Bodø during World War II"]. Lecture, University College of Bodø, September 22, 2008.

Karlsvik. On the Way Home. Directed by Tamara Sushko. Luleå, 2013. Documentary film.

Scissors and Secrets. Directed by Tamara Sushko and Liv Mjelde. Luleå, 2018. Documentary film.

Våganavisa. November 19, 2014.

Thorsen, Thor. "Minner fra Lohmannfabrikken i Hammerfest" ["Memories of the Lohmann Factory in Hammerfest"]. Letter to Roland Hasslich, December 13, 1998.

Årbok for Vågan. Vågan Historielag, 2012, 2013, 2014.

NOTES

Author's Introduction

Page 2: Gunnar D. Hatlehol argues that: Gunnar D. Hatlehol, "Prisoners and Forced Laborers in German Occupied Norway, 1940–1945: A Historiographical Survey," *Arbeiderhistorie* 24, no. 1 (March 2020): 61–83.

Page 2: Krogh self-published his book: Helge Krogh, *Sjette-kolonne--?: Om den norske storindustriens bidrag til Nazi-Tysklands krigføring [The Sixth Column? On Norwegian Industry's Contribution to Nazi Germany's Warfare]* (Pax, 1970).

Chapter 1. "My father was born in Norway"

Page 1: "and I wish you good luck": Dag Skogheim, e-mail, October 11, 2005.

Page 11: "an estimated 13,700 died of starvation and disease": Marianne Neerland Soleim, "Graves of the 'Other': Norway and the

Commemoration of Soviet Prisoners of War," *Heritage, Memory and Conflict* 3 (May 10, 2023): 15–18, https://doi.org/10.3897/hmc.3.71298. This number is derived from the Norwegian War Grave Service and information from German prison cards. There is still uncertainty around these numbers; the Soviet authorities asserted that the number of missing soldiers was 16,000.

Page 12: "memory agents": Steinar Aas, "Norwegian and Soviet/Russian World War II Memory Policy During the Cold War and the Post-Soviet Years," *Acta Borealia* 29, no. 2 (July 2012): 216, https://doi.org/10.1080/08003831.2012.678721.
12 Operation Asphalt: Marianne Neerland Soleim, *"Operasjon Asfalt": Kald krig om krigsgraver* [*"Operation Asphalt": Cold War over War Graves*] (Orkana Akademisk, 2016), https://doi.org/10.33673/ OOA20192.

Page 12: Her groundbreaking doctoral dissertation: Marianne Neerland Soleim, *Sovjetiske krigsfanger i Norge—Antall, organisering og repatriering. Avhandling i historie* [*Soviet Prisoners of War in Norway 1941–1945: Numbers, Organization and Repatriation*], PhD dissertation, Universitetet i Tromsø, 2004.

Chapter 2. Yuri: The Boy with the "Undesirable Background"

Page 18: Rand House bed and breakfast: Now a hotel, it is named after one of St. Petersburg's famous daughters, Alisa Zinovyevna Rosenbaum—better known by her pen name Ayn Rand—who left St. Petersburg for the USA in 1926.

Page 19: "Your parents' past can affect my daughter's future": Olga Kozhemyakina, "«Я родился в немецком плену». Об этом архитектор из Петербурга узнал через 50 лет | Правмир" ["'I was born in German captivity': The artist from St. Petersburg learned about this 50 years later"], *Pravmir.ru*, March 10, 2020. https://www.pravmir.ru/ya-rodilsya-v-nemeczkom-plenu-ob-etom-arhitektor-iz-peterburga-uznal-cherez-50-let/.

Page 21: Silent and afraid, as before the war: Svetlana Alexievich, *The Unwomanly Face of War*, trans. Richard Pevear and Larissa Volokhonsky, 1st ed. (Penguin, 2017).

Page 21: Vladimir Putin has said: Vladimir Vladimirovič Putin and Natalija Pavlovna Gevorkjan, *First Person* (Hutchinson, 2000).

Page 23: "a gigantic act of ethnic cleansing": Neal Acherson, review of *After Seven Hundred Years*, by Max Egremont, *London Review of Books*, May 24, 2012, https://www.lrb.co.uk/the-paper/v34/n10/neal-ascherson/after-seven-hundred-years.

Page 23: There will be no mixture of populations: "POLAND (Hansard, December 15, 1944)," https://api.parliament.uk/historic-hansard/commons/1944/dec/15/poland (accessed May 15, 2024).

Page 23: The Soviets made this ice-free port on the Baltic: See for example CIA, "Lindenau Shipyard in Klaipeda (CIA-RDP82-00457R008100380013-1)," Central Intelligence Agency, September 6, 1951; and Norman Polmar. "Soviet Shipbuilding and Shipyards," *United States Naval Institute Proceedings* 98/5/831 (May 1, 1972).

Chapter 4. Fedor: A Grand Alliance and a Great Betrayal

Page 32: The Molotov–Ribbentrop Pact: Alexander Werth, *Russia at War, 1941–1945* (Dutton, 1964), 74–75.

Page 32: Records from the memorial archives: This information was supplied and translated for us by Elena Badanina, a Russian researcher working at the Narvik Red Cross memorial center, whom we met at the Lulea Memorial in 2015.

Page 33: an unusual performance: Werth, *Russia at War*.

Page 34: Babi Yar: See: Anatoli (Kutnesov) 1970.

Page 35: Fedor was captured on September 24: ID 65741078. Информация из документов, уточняющих потери [Information from documents clarifying losses.] Accessed in the Generalized Computer Data Bank of the Ministry of Defense of the Russian Federation (OBD "Memorial"), https://obd-memorial.ru/html/info.htm?id=65741078

Page 36: A total of 616,000 soldiers surrendered: Micheal Clodfelter, *Warfare and Armed Conflicts: A Statistical Reference to Casualty and Other Figures, 1500–2000*, 2nd ed. (McFarland, 2001).

Page 36: trials and suffering: Hatlehol, "Prisoners and Forced Laborers in German Occupied Norway."

Page 37: the *Monte Rosa*: The *Monte Rosa* was transferred to British ownership as a war prize in 1945. Renamed the *Empire Windrush* after the war, it acquired almost legendary status as the ship that brought some of the earliest Jamaican immigrants to the UK in 1948. Collectively, Caribbean immigrants who came to Britain in the 1940s and 1950s are known as the "Windrush Generation." See Trevor Phillips and Mike Phillips, *Windrush: Seventy-five Years of Modern Britain*, new ed. (Mudlark, 2023).

Page 37: Four transfers from Germany went directly: Ann-Cathrin Braseth and Astrid Borchgrevink, "Sendt til fiendens leir" ["Sent into the Enemy Camp"], in *About Bodø*, Bodø Municipality, 1991. Marianne Neerland Soleim gives an overview of Soviet soldiers' arrival in Norway in the years 1941, 1942, 1943, 1944, 1945. *Final Report. Prisoners of War Executive 1945* (in *Sovjetiske krigsfanger i Norge 1941–1945*, 56).

Chapter 5. Gallina: A City Starved, a Girl Abducted

Page 41: "The iron ring around Leningrad has been closed": Chris Bellamy, *Absolute War: Soviet Russia in the Second World War*, Pan Military Classics. Macmillan, 2007, 351.

Page 41: "erase the city of Petersburg": Chris Bellamy, *Absolute War*, 354–357.

Page 42: There was no food for long periods: Ibid., 372–373.

Page 44: German soldiers had occupied Gzhatsk: The information presented in this section about Gzhatsk during the war years is taken from notes we made at the museum, and subsequent communication with the resident historian.

Chapter 6. The Nordic Countries in Hitler's War

Page 50: "Operation Weserübung": Lars Gyllenhaal and James F. Gebhardt, *Slaget om Nordkalotten* [*The Battle for Nordkalotten*] (Historiska Media, 1999).

Page 51: Sweden also loaned 500 train cars: Gyllenhaal and Gebhardt, *Slaget om Nordkalotten*, 15.

Page 51: The border between the two nations: M. B. Michelet, *Den største forbrytelsen: Ofre og gjerningsmenn i det norske Holocaust* [*The greatest crime: Victims and perpetrators in the Norwegian Holocaust*]. Gyldendal, 2014; M. B. Michelet, *Hva visste hjemmefronten? Holocaust i Norge: varslene, unnvikelsene, hemmeligholdet* [*What Did the Home Front Know? The Holocaust in Norway: The Warnings, the Evasions, the Secrecy*] (Gyldendal, 2018).

Page 52: Norway's resistance movement: P. H. F. Borgen and T. Hofsbro, *Norske polititropper i Sverige/Norge 1943-45: Operasjone i Norge 1944 – 1945* [*Norwegian Police Troops in Sweden/Norway 1943–45: Operations in Norway 1944–1945*] (Veteranforeningens historielag, 2006).

Page 52: Norway's resistance movement: Alf R. Jacobsen, *Hat. Hevn. Håp. Historien om det moderne Norge 1945–2000* [*Hate. Revenge. Hope. The History of Modern Norway 1945–2000*] (Vega forlag, 2015).

Chapter 7. To Feed an Army

Page 53: "Norway's contribution": Vasily Grossman, *A Writer at War: Vasily Grossman with the Red Army 1941–1945*, trans. Antony Beevor and Luba Vinogradova (Pimlico/Random House, 2006), 30.

Page 53: They were vital provisions: Helge Paulsen, "Tysk økonomisk politikk i Norge 1940–45," in *Krigen i Norge* [*The War in Norway*], ed. Hans Fredrik Dahl (Pax, 1974). Bjørn Petter Finstad, "Spiskammer for det tredje riket" ["Larders for the Third Reich"], in *Norges fiskeri og kysthistorie* [*The Norwegian Fishery and Coastal History*], ed. Nils Kolle et al. (Akademisk Forlag, 2014).

Page 54: The work of the German political thinker Carl Schmitt:Tracy Strong, "Introduction" in Carl Schmitt, *The Concept of the Political: Expanded Edition*, ed. George Schwab (University of Chicago Press, 2007). See also Thomas Meany, "So It Must Be for Ever," *London Review of Books*, July 14, 2016: 5.

Page 55: fish and energy: Alan S. Milward, "Fascism and the Economy," in *Fascism: A Reader's Guide*, ed. Walter Laqueur (Penguin, 1976); Alan S. Milward, *The Fascist Economy in Norway* (Clarendon Press, 1972).

Page 55: in a letter to Josef Terboven: Paulsen, "Tysk økonomisk," 1974: 80; see also Strategikakos, 2020.
Page 55: He regarded Norway and Norwegians: Terje Emberland and Matthew Kott, *Himmlers Norge: Nordmenn i det storgermanske prosjekt* [*Himmler's Norway: Norwegians in the Greater-Germanic Project*] (Aschehoug, 2012). See also Milward, "Fascism and the Economy," 444.

Page 56: an agreement was reached: Paulsen, "Tysk økonomisk," 85.

Page 56: The Reichskommissariat: Bjørn Petter Finstad, "The Norwegian Fishing Sector during the German Occupation: Continuity or Change?" in *Industrial Collaboration in Nazi-Occupied Europe: Norway in*

Context, ed. Hans Otto Frøland, Mats Ingulstad, and Jonas Scherner. 389–415 (Palgrave Macmillan, 2016), 396.

Page 57: the corporation Frostfilet A/S was formally established: "Frostfilet A/S" and "A/S Frostfilet" are both used in requests to the government. In Trondheim, "Frostfilet A/S" was used on the stationary heading.

Page 57: Even before its formal establishment: National Archives, Trondheim, Box 578, Customs Department. Letter to the Finance and Customs Department of July 19, 1940. The letter states that the business was started June 6 with equipment already acquired.

Page 57: Frostfilet had its roots: Bjørn Nilsen, *Altså egentlig n' Nekolai: historia om oppfinneren, sildegrossisten og originalen Nekolai Dahl* [*Actually, It's n' Nekolai: The Story of the Inventor, Herring Wholesaler and Original Nekolai Dahl*] (Steinbit Forlag, 2006).

Page 57: Additionally, twenty Germans were working: Hans Jürgen Kahle, *Verschleppt nach Cuxhaven: Eine Dokumentation über das Schicksal der ausländischen Arbeiter und Kriegsgefangenen in Cuxhaven, im Kreis Land Hadeln und dem Landkreis Wesermünde während der Zeit des Nationalsozialismus* [*Carried Away into the Cuxhaven Night: Documenting the Fate of Foreign Workers and Prisoners of War in Cuxhaven, Kreis Land Hadeln Province, and Wesermünde (Bremerhaven) during the Time of National Socialism*] (Wilhelm-Heidsiek Verlag, 1995).

Page 58: the factory's primary objective: Morten Strand, *St. Petersburg-historier* [*St. Petersburg Stories*] (Tiden Norsk Forlag, 2005), 215.

Page 58: eight shipments of frozen cod and pollock: National Archives, Trondheim, Box 578.

Chapter 8. To Remake an Industry

Page 59: The Reichskommissariat's first annual report: Milward, "Fascism and the Economy," 34; cited in Bjorn Petter Finstad, *Fiskerinæringen i Finnmark under okkupasjonen* [*The Fishing Industry in Finnmark During the Occupation*] (unpublished MA thesis, University of Tromsø, 1993).

Page 60: the importance they placed on primary commodities: Emberland and Kott, *Himmlers Norge*, 61.

Page 60: These firms invested fully or in part: Milward, "Fascism and the Economy," 35; cited in Finstad, *Fiskerinæringen i Finnmark.*

Page 61: rules of *Fischeinkauf*: Milward, "Fascism and the Economy," 36; cited in Finstad, *Fiskerinæringen i Finnmark.*
Page 61: "Freighter captains are like camel owners": Interview with Torbjørn Feiring, who worked at Frostfilet/ Langstranda in the spring of 1945

Page 61: profiting considerably: Pamphlet in the Gunnerius library archive, Trondheim. "To the Fishermen. Signed Neptun." February 3, 1945. Private archive no. 19. War time archive xi NTNU UB .

Page 62: the Schjølberg brothers: Archives in Nordland, Bodø, Box 001. Ragnar Schjølberg.

Page 63: It also housed a cod-liver oil steam extractor: Strand, *St. Petersburg-historier*, 214.

Page 63: Unilever became a partner with Nordsee: Finstad, "Spiskammer for det tredje riket," 373.

Page 63: it benefited from investments: These paradoxes and dilemmas were clearly described during the Second World War. See J. Kuczynski and M. Witt, *The Economics of Barbarism: Hitler's New Economic Order in Europe* (Frederick Muller, 1942); Joseph Borkin and Charles A. Welsh, *Germany's Master Plan: The Story of Industrial Offensive* (Duell, Sloan & Pearce, 1943).

Page 66: The processed fish was packed: Finstad, "Spiskammer for det tredje riket," 373-374.

Page 66: The war brought rapid expansion: Liv Mjelde, *Apprenticeship: From Practice to Theory and Back Again* (University of Joensuu Publications in Social Sciences No. 19, 1993), 72.

Page 67: Employment in the fishing industry: Finstad 1993, 133.

Page 67: Norwegians were ordered to register for work: Gunnar D. Hatlehol, *"Norwegeneinsatz" 1940–1945: Organisation Todts arbeidere i Norge og graden av tvang ["The Norwegian Effort," 1940–1945: Organisation Todt's Workers in Norway and Degrees of Coercion]* (NTNU, 2015).

Page 67: "worst among the newly arrived workers": Linda Helen Haukland, *Hverdag i ruinene [Ruins of Everyday Life]* (Orkana Akademisk, 2012), 195–99.

Page 67: German records from the period: Nordland Archives, Box 0011. Bodø.

Page 67: *Cuxhaven Tagesblatt*: Kahle, quoted in Finstad, "Spiskammer for det tredje riket," 373.

Chapter 9. The Female Labor Conundrum: Ideology vs. Pragmatism

Page 69: Kittner raised the issue: National Archives, Trondheim. Box Æa 02, Øa 01. County Commissioner for Norland. Frostfilet Langstranda—Bodø.

Page 71: This intention was confirmed: This data is based on letters sent from the Frostfilet department in Bodø to various Norwegian and German authorities between 19/5 1941 and 22/11 1943. I have received a copy of the letters from Knut Støre.

Page 71: the concepts of women's equality: George L. Mosse, *Nazi Culture: Intellectual, Cultural and Social Life in the Third Reich* (Schocken Books, 1981).

Page 72: biology was destiny: Carl Müller Frøland's book *The Nazi Idea-universe* (Vidarforlaget, 2017) contributes to our understanding of the basis for the rise of Nazism. See also Renate Bridenthal et al. (eds.), *When Biology Became Destiny: Women in Weimar and Nazi Germany* (Monthly Review Press, 1984), and Bernt L. Otterstad's article "Eugenikkrati (Eugenicracy)," *Klassekampen*, May 13, 2017.

Page 72: The so-called granting of equal rights: Translated in K. M. Offen, *European Feminisms, 1700-1950: A Political History* (Stanford University Press, 2000).

Page 72: historian Claudia Koonz argued: C. Koonz, *Mothers in the Fatherland: Women, the Family, and Nazi Politics*, 1st ed. (St. Martin's Press, 1987).

Page 73: the Nasjonal Samling: See Finn Jørgen Solberg, *Liste Nr. 1 over mistenkte for grovere arter av landsvik. Mai 1945* (Vega forlag, 2014).

Page 74: These homes housed Norwegian women: Sabine Lee, *Children Born of War in the Twentieth Century* (Oxford University Press, 2017).

Page 74: These homes housed Norwegian women: Daša Drndić, *Trieste* (Houghton Mifflin Harcourt, 2012).

Page 74: "Norway, where this was a flourishing activity": Drndić, *Trieste*.

Page 76: "there was a clear expectation": Dag Ellingsen, *Living Conditions of Norwegian War Children*, Statistics Norway, September 26, 2023.

Page 76: the case was later dismissed: Petra Tabeling, "Children of Shame – Norway's Dark Secret," Deutsche-Welle, December 2, 2001.

https://www.dw.com/en/children-of-shame-norways-dark-secret/a-336916.

Page 76: "Norwegian authorities violated": Iliana Magra, "Norway Apologizes, 70 Years Later, to Women Who Had Relationships with WWII Germans," *The New York Times*, October 19, 2018, sec. World. https://www.nytimes.com/2018/10/19/world/europe/norway-lebensborn-german-girls.html.

Page 76: Women have been part: Miriam Glucksmann, *Women Assemble: Women Workers and the New Industries in Inter-War Britain* (Routledge, 1990); Liv Mjelde, "Kjønn, arbeidsdeling og forandring i den grafiske bedriften" ["Gender, Division of Labor and Change in the Printing Industry"], in *Arbeidsdeling i en brytningstid*, ed. Liv Mjelde and A. L. Tarrou (Gyldendal, 1992); Linda Cullum, "Whose Interest? Women Organizing on the Waterfront—St. Johns, Newfoundland," *Journal of Historical Sociology* 22, no. 1 (2009): 71–96.

Page 77: The struggle for women's right: Liv Mjelde, "Bygningsarbeid, mannfolk yrke eller?" ["Building Trades, Men's Work, or…?"], in *Kvinnens årbok* [*Women's Yearbook*] (Pax, 1975); Mjelde, 1992.

Page 77: In northern Norway: Marit Husmo, "Gender and Total Quality Management: The Quality Assurance Process in Norwegian Fish Processing," in *Global Coasts: Life Changes, Gender Challenges* (1999); see also Cullum, "Whose Interest?"

Page 78: Approximately 1.3 million prisoners: Alex de Waal, "The Nazis Used It, We Use It," *London Review of Books*, June 14, 2017. https://www.lrb.co.uk/the-paper/v39/n12/alex-de-waal/the-nazis-used-it-we-use-it.

Chapter 10. The "Eastern Workers" Arrive

Page 83: Many individuals from both groups: Michael Stokke, *Sovjetiske og franske sivilarbeidere i Norge 1942–1945: En sammenligning av* *arbeids- og leveforhold* [*Soviet and French Civilian Workers in Norway 1942–45*], master's thesis, University of Bergen, 2008, 29.

Page 83: the County Commissioner: National Archives, Trondheim, Box Æa 02, Øa 01. County Commissioner for Nordland. Frostfilet Langstranda, Nordland.

Page 83: They vary from one document to the next: Regarding the number of workers, I have relied on data obtained from descriptions in German correspondence. Regarding the description of the working conditions, I have relied on material provided by Knut Støre and Arkiv Nordland, interviews of people who were present in Bodø in 1945 and on the research projects of Dag Andreassen and Bjørn-Petter Finstad. Another source is the descriptions provided by the women themselves and Norwegians that worked together with them (see also Magne Haugland, *Do Svidania—På gjensyn: Dokumentarberetninger om sovjetiske krigsfanger* [*Do Svidania—Goodbye: Documented Accounts of Soviet Prisoners of War*] (Commentum Forlag, 2008).

Page 84: The majority were Russians: Haugland, *Do Svidania—På gjensyn*, 9.

Page 86: While most of the women: Kahle, *Verschleppt nach Cuxhaven.*

Page 86: Many were opposed: Alexievich, *The Unwomanly Face of War*, 238–39.

Chapter 12. Life Behind Barbed Wire

Page 98: "The Russians stole from the warehouses": Archive Nordland, Box E001, the Schjølberg Archive.

Page 98: widespread subversion and theft: Arkiv Nordland, Box EE 0011, the Schølberg Archive. Accounts by Ragnar Schølberg.

Page 99: Norwegian Hird guards: Braaseth and Borchgrevink, *"Sendt til fiendens leir,"* 75.

Page 100: The entire cargo was returned: Knut Støre, private archive.

Page 100: The first act of sabotage: Arkiv Nordland, Box EE 0011, the Schjølberg Archive. The account of Ragnar Schjølberg.

Page 100: a tragic accident: Michael Stokke's private archives. An undated list of burials in Bodø County shows ten persons. Five worked at *Frostfilet* (Langstranda). Anna Mischufkina was the only woman.

Page 100: documents describe acts of sabotage: Dag Andreassen, referring to minutes from the factory. Dag Andreassen, *Kjøle og fryseteknologi: fra planer til industri. Den norsk-tyske filetfabrikk på Melbu 1940–45* [*Cooling and Freezer Technology from Plans to Industry: The Norwegian–German Fish-Fillet Plant at Melbu 1940–45*] (Universitetet i Bergen, 1995), 95.

Page 100: Research by Dag Andreassen: Dag Andreassen, *Kjøle og fryseteknologi.*

Chapter 13. Marfa: Work, Resistance, and Love

Page 105: "They really longed": Kozhemyakina, "«Я родился в немецком плену»."

Page 106: *In 1941, my mother's family*: Michael Stokke gave me a copy of this letter from Valentina Stepina. The letter was translated to Norwegian on March 3, 2008, by Tatiana A. Sphak. I interviewed Valentina Stepina in Luleå in May 2015.

Page 106: *The other girls were grumpy*: Interview with Marfa Maksimova, received from Michael Stokke, January 15, 2015. Tamara Sushko (2013) interview with Marfa Maksimova in the documentary *Karlsvik: On the Road Home* (Luleå).

Page 107: Similar photographs have been found: Magne Haugland also collected photographs of Soviet prisoners from all over the country in his 2008 book *Do Svidania—På gjensyn*.

Page 109: A telegram dated September 12, 1942: Trondheim National Archives, Box Æe 02, Nordland County Commissioner.

Page 109: Vladimir Kozlov: Haugland, *Do Svidania—På gjensyn*, 407–412.

Page 110: "The Casablanca of the North": A. Skjeseth, *Nordens Casablanca: Nordmenn i Stockholm under krigen* [*The Casablanca of the North: Norwegians in Stockholm during the War*] (Spartacus, 2018).

Page 110: The first Norwegian woman: Astrid Meland, "Sjarmert til spionasje" ["Charmed into espionage"], *Dagbladet*, April 27, 2004, sec. magasinet. https://www.dagbladet.no/magasinet/sjarmert-til-spionasje/65961967.

Chapter 14. Anny: The Girl Who Stayed

Page 111: The roster included: Kahle, *Verschleppt nach Cuxhaven*.

Page 112: Trained as a seamstress: Annemarie Lorentzen, *Fra Ukraina-en gang verdens kornkammer- til verdens nordligste by* [*From Ukraine—Once the World's Grain Silo—to the World's Northernmost City*] (Øyfolk. Nr. 8, Hammerfest historielag, 1997).

Page 113: *Prinsesse Ragnhild*: Museum Nord, "SS *Prinsesse Ragnhild*, the Worst War Time Ship Wreck," Museum Nord. Accessed March 13, 2025, https://www.museumnord.no/en/stories/ss-princess-ragnhild-norwegians-and-germans-in-the-same-boat/.

Page 114: Vereinigte Tiefkühlgesellschaft Lohmann & Co.: Finstad 1993; Lorentzen, "Fra Ukraina"; Stokke, *Sovjetiske og franske sivilarbeidere*.

114 pioneers of Norway's frozen fish industry: Jacobsen, *Fra brent jord til Klondyke* [*From Scorched Earth to Klondike*] (Universitetsforlaget, 1996), 18; Finstad, "Spiskammer for det tredje riket."

Page 114: *"I remember the painful and somber atmosphere"*: This article was sent to Roland Masslich in Bremen on December 13, 1998, who passed it on to me.

Page 115: *"Freien nach Osten"*: Jacobsen, *Fra brent jord til Klondyke,* 22.

Page 115: He was responsible for the health: Dr. Spiering left diary notes about his experiences in Norway. A copy of one page of the diary about the Ukrainian women is reproduced in Anders Gogstad's article "50 års minne, sett fra den andre siden. En tysk kollegas inntrykk fra sine år i Norge som militærlege 1940–1945," *Tidsskrift for den norske legeforening* 115, no. 30 (1995): 3765–3767.

Page 116: All the women were sent: Michael Stokke's private archive.

Page 117: Holger later remarked: Thor Thorsen, "Erinnerungen an die Lohmann-fabrik in Hammerfest" ["Memories of the Lohmann Factory in Hammerfest"], *Trollposten JG.* 6, nos. 2 and 3 (2000).

Chapter 15. Daily Life and a Strike

Page 119: During their first winter: *Finnmarks Dagblad*, 11/7, 1984; Thorsen, "Erinnerungen an die Lohmann-fabrik in Hammerfest."

Page 121: Dr. Riel, wrote to the authorities: The writer Alf R. Jacobsen refers to a report dated February 8, 1944, in his book *Fra Brent Jord til Klondike,* which he translated from German. Jacobsen grew up in Hammerfest, and says he was and is surprised by the silence that is around the Lohmann factory, which was the major production factory in Hammerfest between 1941 and 1944.

Page 122: *I am personally of the opinion*: Jacobsen, *Fra Brent Jord til Klondike*, 22–23.

Page 122: Organisation Todt had its offices: Interview with Svein Schou, December 8, 2014. He was an errand boy in Oslo in 1945, and delivered merchandise to 6 Dronningens Street.
122 Holms Hotel in Geilo: Personal communication by e-mail from Michael Stokke, March 16, 2016.

Page 123: "minor war": Lars Westerlund, "Utländska soldater och unga kvinnor under andra världskriget: Kulturmöten i Västeuropa och råhet i Östeuropa; moderniseringsvånda i Nordfinland och på Island" ["Foreign Soldiers and Young Women during World War II: Cultural Encounter in Western Europe and Brutality in Eastern Europe; the Agony of Modernization in Northern Finland and on Iceland"]. *Tornedalens årsbok*, no. 14 (2011), 65.

Page 123: "impure bastards": Westerlund, "Utländska soldater," 65.

Page 123: Anny and Jacob married: Lorentzen, *Fra Ukraina*, 83.

Chapter 16. Finnmark on Fire

Page 128: "Sword of Stalingrad": Grossman, *A Writer at War*, 2006; Grossman, *Stalingrad*, 2019.

Page 129: "Miracle of Litsa": Alf R. Jacobsen, *Miraklet ved Lista: Hitlers første nederlag på Østfronten* [*Miracle at Lista: Hitler's First Defeat on the Eastern Front*] (Vega Forlag, 2014), 55.

Page 129: An estimated fifty to seventy thousand soldiers: Jacobsen, *Miraklet ved Lista*, 55.

Page 130: They wanted to fight: Bruce Myles, *Night Witches: The Amazing Story of Russia's Women Pilots in World War II* (Panther Books, 1983).

Page 130: Nazi soldiers likened the sound: Myles, *Night Witches*, 60.

Page 130: The bravery and fortitude: See also K. S. Karol, *Solik: Life in the Soviet Union, 1939–1946* (Pluto Press, 1983).

Page 130: The bravery and fortitude: See Kazimiera Janin Cottam, *Women in War: Selected Biography of Soviet Women Soldiers* (Focus, 1998) for more information.

Page 130: Tone had it published: Anne Helskog, *Det er bombevær i natt: Fire år i Festung Kirkenes* [*It's Bombing Weather Tonight: Four Years in Fortress Kirkenes*] (Bealljecohkka, 2006), 141.

Page 131: *"They certainly fully share the hardships"*: Helskog, *Det er bombevær i natt*, 141.

Page 132: It means murder and plunder: Henrik Nordhus, *Kirkenes i krigsåra 1940–1945. Kirkenes brannvesen og Det sivile luftverns beretning* [*Kirkenes During the War Years 1940–1945. Kirkenes Fire Department and Civil Air Defense Report*] (Sør-Varanger kommune, 1948). See also Helskog, *Det er bombevær i natt*.

Page 132: 'Iron Curtain' will fall: Helskog, *Det er bombevær i natt*, 120.

Page 132: A February announcement: NTNU, UB, private archive No. 19, The War Archive x1. Fishery. February 3, 1945, 19.3.45.

Page 133: A report on the scorched-earth destruction: Karen Hunt, *The World Transformed, 1914–1945* (Pearson, 2014), 104.

Page 133: All buildings were to be completely vacated: Dag Skogheim, *Med slukte lanterner* [*With Lanterns Snuffed Out*] (Gjenreisningsmuseet for Finnmark og Nord-Troms, 1998), 26–27.

Chapter 17. Evacuation

Page 135: According to Dr. Gustav Vig: Skogheim, *Med slukte lanterner,* 27.

Page 136: "heard that there were four dead in the chapel": The chapel was one of the few buildings in Hammerfest that was not burned down.

Page 137: She joined a group of Frostfilet workers: Haukland, *Hverdag i ruinene,* 232.

Page 137: Although it did not explode: Haukland, *Hverdag i ruinene,* 192–93.

Page 138: collection of objects made by Soviet prisoners: See also Soleim, *"Operasjon asphalt."* Guttorm Guttormsgaard showed the work by Russian prisoners of war in an exposition entitled "Om verdighet" (*On Dignity*) in 2012.

Page 138: this museum is the first in Norway: See also Marianne Neerland Soleim, Jens-Ivar Nergård, and Oddmund Andersen, *Grenselos i grenseland* [*Borderless in Bordelands*] (Orkana Akademisk, 2015).

Page 139: The townspeople provided: Eva Rosenberg, "Englandsturen" ["Tour of England"], in *Årbok for Vågan* (Skolp, 2014), 82–83.

Page 139: "It was a sinister and frightening sight": Andersen, 2014:39.

Page 140: decipher future German war plans: Cato Guhnfeldt, "Lofotraidet fikk et uventet utbytte" ["Unexpected Payoff to the Lofot Raid"], *Aftenposten,* March 16, 2016.

Page 141: "Svolvær hostages": William Hakvaag, *De utrolige bildene* [*Unbelievable Pictures*] (Kolofon Forlag, 2013), 150–51.

Page 141: "zone of destiny in this war": Despina Stratigakos, *Hitler's Northern Utopia: Building the New Order in Occupied Norway* (Princeton University Press, 2020), 6.

Page 141: Remnants of the massive fortifications: Strategigakos, *Hitler's Northern Utopia*, 6.

Chapter 18. Final Stop: From Svolvær to Langstranda

Page 144: "fish guano" factory: Ishita Ahuja et al., Fish and Fish Waste-Based Fertilizers in Organic Farming—With Status in Norway: A Review," *Waste Management* 115 (September 1, 2020): 95–112.

Page 145: Although all the fish-freezing machinery: Erling and Anny's information differs on this point from that of researchers. Finstad's opinion was that production was started on Svinøya.

Page 145: Sixty were sent: These numbers are not verified. We have not been able to trace the sixty women who supposedly were sent to Trondheim. There was nothing in the archives in Trondheim. We have our information from Anny Evensen.

Page 146: they obtained the same status: Stokke, *Sovjetiske og franske sivilarbeidere*, 43.

Page 146: the Nazis could see defeat coming: Ole-Jacob Abraham, "Russarfangene—mytar, fakta og nyanser" ["Russian Prisoners: Myths, Facts, and Nuances"], *Historisk Tidsskrift*, no. 2 (2009); Einar Kr. Steffenak, *Russerfangene: Sovjetiske krigsfanger i Norge og deres skjebne* [*Russian Prisoners: Soviet Prisoners of War in Norway and Their Fate*] (Humanist Forlag, 2008); Stokke, *Sovjetiske og franske sivilarbeidere.*

Page 146: Jonni was born: Nordland Archives, Box Milorg in Nordland. Undated letter signed Bolstad.

Page 148: In total, forced laborers received: Stokke, *Sovjetiske og franske sivilarbeidere.*

Chapter 19. The Reich Collapses

Page 152: The country's leading conservative newspaper: See Bjørn Westlie, *Det norske jødehatet. Propaganda og Presse under okkupasjonen [Norway's Anti-Semitism: Propaganda and Press during the Occupation]* (Res Publica, 2019).

Page 153: Major General Roy Urquhart arrived: Jacobsen, *Hat. Hevn. Håp*, 155.

Page 153: the ceremony at Reims: Valentin Berezhkov, *History in the Making: Memoirs of World War II Diplomacy* (Progress Publishers, 1982), 434–35.

Page 154: around 350,000 German soldiers remained: Jacobsen, *Hat. Hevn. Håp*, 26-27.

Page 154: avalanche of retribution: Carmen Callill, *Bad Faith: A Story of Family and Fatherland* (Vintage, 2007).

Page 154: An estimated 45,000 Norwegian: Thomas V. H. Hagen, "Nordmenn i fangenskap under andre verdenskrig" ["Norwegians in Captivity during World War II"], in *Nordmenn i fangenskap 1940—1945* (Universitetsforlag, 2004).

Page 154: local plans were also made: For a general discussion of the Norwegian resistance movement in English, see O. Riste and B. Nøkleby, *Norway 1940-45: The Resistance Movement*, 3rd ed. (Aschehoug, 1994).

Chapter 20. Langstranda Liberated

Page 156: Dr. Johnson's mettle was put to the test: Archive Nordland, Box D 0001 Milorg. Notes from the Olav Angell memoir about the German capitulation in May 1945. (Puerto de la Cruz, May 1995.)

Page 156: Among these workers was Jacob Evensen: Nordland Archives, Box Milorg in Nordland. Undated letter signed Bolstad.

Page 156: prison camp at Langstranda: Egil Ulateig quotes from the diary of one Greta Dahl in Narvik, which cites May 7 as the day peace arrived; Egil Ulateig, *Freden: 8. Mai 1945*, 1st ed. (Bergen: Vigmostad & Bjørke, 2015).

Page 156: Allied High Command: Anton Johnson. Archive Nordland, Box D 0001, Milorg D 0002. Milorg in Nordland.

Page 157: "capos": Soleim, *Sovjetiske krigsfanger i Norge*, 130.

Page 157: "Vlasov sympathizers": Werth, *Russia at War*, 649.

Page 157: He defected to the German side: See *Harstad Tidende* (*Harstad Times*), March 28, 1943, "Soviet General Encourages the Soviet Russians to Fight against the 'Red Oppressors'."

Page 158: *At Frostfilet A/S, the Russian forced laborers had*: Leiv Kreyberg, *Frigjøringen av de allierte krigsfangene i Nordland i 1945: En redegjørelse* [*An Account of Freeing the Allies' Prisoners of War in Nordland in 1945*] (Tanum, 1946), 34.

Page 158: At the Moscow Conference in September 1944: Ian Buruma, *Year Zero: A History of 1945* (Atlantic Books, 2013), 150.

Page 159: Stalin's amnesty declaration: Alexievich, *The Unwomanly Face of War*, 76.

Page 159: "Stalin's cruel joke on the political prisoners": Anne Applebaum, *Iron Curtain: The Crushing of Eastern Europe, 1944–1956* (Penguin, 2012). Solzhenitsyn was originally sentenced under Article 58 of the Soviet criminal code, for spreading "anti-Soviet propaganda" after questioning Stalin's leadership in a personal letter to a friend.

Page 161: The Germans left Langstranda: Archive Nordland, Box D0002, Milorg in Nordland.

Page 161: the Norwegian authorities encouraged: Kreyberg, *Frigjøringen av de allierte krigsfangene.*

Page 161: Norway's Constitution Day: Norway became an independent nation in 1905, after hundreds of years being a colony, first under Denmark and then from 1814 until 1905, under Sweden.

Page 161: *"With capitulation we found ourselves"*: Archive Nordland, Box D 0002, Milorg in Nordland. Letter to Milorg in Nordland.

Page 162: *"The factory has been broken into"*: Archive Nordland, Box D 0002, Milorg in Nordland.

Page 162: The Royal Navy arrived: Jacobsen, *Hat. Hevn. Håp.*

Chapter 21. "Until We Meet Again"

Page 163: They had showers at the factory: Eight forced laborers were listed as dead at Frostfilet, Langstranda, during the war (personal communication, e-mail Michael Stokke, December 15, 2017).

Page 164: mass transportation, interrogation, and delousing: Kreyberg, *Frigjøringen av de allierte krigsfangene,* 10.

Page 164: he wanted the camps organized: Ibid.
165: The Germans must be treated: Archive Nordland, Box D 0002,

Milorg. Letter from Kreyberg to Second Lieutenant Haakenaasen F.S.H.I.

Page 166: "lost fathers": Also, the former intelligence officer Per Jevne, a fluent Russian speaker, has spent his retirement years helping former prisoners to find relatives in Norway. See B. Wormdal, "Tyskerbarna fikk erstatning—hvorfor kan ikke vi russerbarn få det?" ["The German Children Got Compensation, Why Can't We Russian Children Get It?"], NRK, August 5, 2020. https://www.nrk.no/tromsogfinnmark/krever-oppreisning-for-russerbarna_-slik-tyskerbarna-fikk-1.15109146

Page 167: "Then Lofoten will have been emptied": Captain Nøkleby, report of June 19.

Page 167: in Oslo, 178 women and four children: According to a letter dated March 22, 1945, from the Lohmann factory in Svolvær to the *Reichskommisariat* in Oslo, 99 of the 278 female workers from the East from Hammerfest were sent directly to Bodø and Trondheim. One of the women had married a Russian from the Vlasov Army and two had been brought to an unknown location by the security services. On Svinøya in March 1945, there were 178 women and 4 children, according to Michael Stokke's private archive.

Page 167: a total of 24,494 prisoners of war: Gunnar Grytås, *Malmtunge spor: Historia om Ofotbanen* [*Heavy Tracks of Iron Ore: History of the Ofot Railway*] (Det Norske Samlaget, 2017), 208.

Page 167: Of these, 424 were women: The numbers in Grytås' book do not tally with the numbers from Luleå which state 24,339, while Grytås states 24,494 – a difference of 55 persons.

Chapter 22. Valentina: A Childhood Under a Cloud

Page 170: she took temporary jobs: Letter from Valentina Stepina to Michael Stokke, 2008. Tamara Sushko's interview with Valentina

Stepina and her mother and with Valentina Nicolaevna Lakutina (2013, *Karslvik: On the Way Home*). Our interview with Valentina Stepina in Boden, Sweden, May 8, 2015. See also the film documentary by Tamara Sushko and Liv Mjelde, *Secrets and Scissors*.

Chapter 23. A Gathering in Luleå

Page 180: "Do not hate": See Gyllenhal & Gebhardt, *Slaget om Nord-kalotten*, 169–180.

Page 180: "memory politics": Steinar Aas, "Norwegian and Soviet/Russian World War II Memory Policy During the Cold War and the Post-Soviet Years," *Acta Borealia* 29, no. 2, (July 2012): 216, https://doi.org/10.1080/08003831.2012.678721.

Page 181: the work of Marianne Neerland Soleim: Soleim *"Operasjon asfalt."*

Page 182: "The topic was forbidden": Kozhemyakina, "«Я родился в немецком плену»."

Page 184: Bodø's mayor approved the idea: *Avisa Nordland* [*Nordland Newspaper*], May 22, 2015: 7. The former mayor, Ida Pinnerød has also approved of the project. We met her when we were launching the Norwegian book in Bodø in September 2018.

Afterword: Researching This Book

Page 186: the sociologist Dorothy E. Smith: See for example: Dorothy E. Smith, *The Everyday World as Problematic: A Feminist Sociology* (University of Toronto Press, 1987).

Page 186: voices like Philip Corrigan:For an introduction to Corrigan's thinking, see *Social Forms/Human Capacities (RLE Social Theory): Essays* *in Authority and Difference* (Routledge, 1990, reissued in 2020). See also the journal *Sociology Lens*, formerly the *Journal of Historical Sociology*, which he co-founded in 1988.

INDEX

www.ingramcontent.com/pod-product-compliance
Lightning Source LLC
Chambersburg PA
CBHW021227130626
46554CB00004B/1395

* 9 7 9 8 9 9 0 6 2 9 3 6 3 *